CONFIDENTLY PARENTING ADHD CHILDREN: PRACTICAL TIPS AND GUIDANCE

GAIN UNDERSTANDING AND CONTROL OVER NEGATIVE BEHAVIOR, ELEVATE COMMUNICATION, AND STRENGTHEN FAMILY BONDS WHILE REDUCING STRESS

MARSHALL VAUGHN

TABLE OF CONTENTS

INTRODUCTION

> *It's not only children who grow. Parents do, too. As much as we watch to see what our children do with their lives, they are watching us to see what we do with ours. I can't tell my children to reach for the sun. All I can do is reach for it, myself.*
>
> JOYCE MAYNARD

Parenting is an extraordinary blend of privilege and responsibility woven together into a tapestry of love and joy. It's a journey where every milestone, from the first hesitant step to the heartfelt exchange of wisdom, carries profound significance.

The privilege lies in witnessing the miracle of a life unfolding, to nurture a tiny soul into a fully-fledged individual brimming with potential and possibility. Yet, alongside this privilege comes the weighty responsibility of guiding, protecting, and shaping that precious life.

It's a role that demands patience, empathy, and unwavering dedication. However, this journey becomes taxing when your child has ADHD. A double helping of patience is required, a deeper understanding of your child's challenges needs to be gained, and sometimes, you dedicate more of yourself to your child than you do for yourself.

However, amidst the challenges and uncertainties, an undeniable beauty permeates the journey. It's found in the tender moments of connection, the laughter that fills the air, and the overwhelming sense of pride accompanying each small triumph.

It's within the excitement in their eyes when they explore and satiate their curiosities, their laughter as they act silly, and in the moments when you know within your heart that you've made a stride in being their parent and helping them navigate the world. Most of all, it's in the moments when you're free of the judgmental and unsolicited advice and criticisms from others because you know in your heart of hearts that your child will thrive and that they are happy, cared for, and loved.

Parenting is a testament to the resilience of the human spirit and the boundless capacity to love. Parenting a child with ADHD is a journey that unfolds unexpectedly, teaching profound lessons of compassion, patience, resilience, and finding the silver lining after every storm.

Your journey may have you tumbling and stumbling at times. You find yourself uncertain and doubting your abilities to be a good parent. You wonder whether something you did wrong has brought about the challenges you're facing as a parent. You shy away from public gatherings and parent groups in fear of the unsolicited advice and criticism that may come your way.

It's an uphill battle trying to get educators and health care professionals on the same page when it comes to your ADHD child and in providing a conducive environment for them to thrive. Deep within these doubts and uncertainty, you feel alone in your challenges.

As a parent of a child with ADHD, every day presents a new set of challenges, from managing impulsivity to helping your child channel their boundless energy in constructive ways. This journey can often feel isolating. However, you're not alone in your experiences and feelings. You're not alone in your doubts, struggles, and uncertainties. Within this book, you'll find a companion, guide, and wealth of knowledge to help you understand and manage your child's ADHD and prioritize your emotional and mental well-being.

This guide provides a comprehensive understanding of ADHD in children, exploring various holistic approaches, evidence-based strategies, and practical exercises. By delving into the perspectives of children with ADHD, the guide enables parents to enhance their communication skills and develop personalized behavior management techniques. With its wide range of resources and insights, this guide offers a valuable roadmap to help parents navigate the complexities of raising a child with ADHD and promote their overall well-being.

More importantly, there is a focus on the importance of self-care for parents and how this relates to the dynamics of parenting your ADHD child. By the end, you feel more confident and better equipped to handle the challenges of parenting an ADHD child, resulting in a more harmonious home environment, enhanced family dynamics, a more empathetic bond between you and your child, and a prioritization of your well-being to build resilience.

Before this guide, your family life may have resembled a turbulent sea, constantly rippling with unpredictable storms. Each day felt like a battle against the relentless tide of exhaustion and frustration. Communication was strained. There was a constant hum of meltdowns and misunderstandings buzzing underneath the roof of your house. Routines were forgotten, and the family was left drifting out to sea.

Then, along the horizon, a light called out to you in the storm, guiding you toward calmer waters. With dedication and perseverance, you've implemented the strategies and exercises tailored to your child's unique needs. Structured routines brought order to the chaos, steadily anchoring the family. Communication blossomed, and a calmness started to settle the once turbulent storm.

Whether you're just beginning to explore this terrain or seeking fresh perspectives on your ongoing journey, this book is your trusted companion, offering a roadmap illuminated by personal experience and expert knowledge. With empathy as the compass and resilience as the guide, you'll embark on this voyage knowing you're not alone, empowered to embrace the full spectrum of your child's potential and provide a home environment filled with understanding, love, and growth. So, dear reader, if you're ready to find companionship, understanding, and empowerment, I invite you to delve deeper, turn the page, and continue your expedition. For within these words lies the promise of hope, empowerment, and a less turbulent and chaotic life for both you and your family.

CHAPTER ONE

EMBRACING THE ADHD MIND
A JOURNEY OF UNDERSTANDING

 *Anyone who exhibits the classic symptoms of ADHD will have difficulty with all or most of the seven core executive functions.*

RUSSEL BARKLEY, PH.D.

As Russell Barkley put so elegantly, ADHD affects not only one's behavior but also one's executive function related to cognitive abilities. One's ability to think adaptively, plan, monitor and control oneself, manage one's time effectively, and organize are all aspects that ADHD impacts due to its impact on cognitive abilities such as attention, memory, perception, logic, reasoning, processing, and mobility. This sets the stage for holistically understanding ADHD and emphasizes the importance of gaining a deeper understanding of this neurodevelopmental disorder.

WHAT IS ADHD?

Attention-deficit/hyperactivity disorder (ADHD) is a condition in which the brain's growth and development are affected (neurodevelopmental disorder). It's one of the most common disorders in children, and once diagnosed in a child, it follows them into adulthood. According to the Centers for Disease Control and Prevention (CDC), an estimated 6 million (9.8%) children aged 3 to 17 have ever been diagnosed with ADHD (2023). Children and Adults with Attention-Deficit/Hyperactivity Disorder (CHADD), on the other hand, estimated that around 129 million children around the world have ADHD (2024). This data reveals a truth we might not have been paying attention to. ADHD is common, and for every child that has ADHD, there is a parent who is navigating those troubling waters, trying to be the best possible parent for the child.

Causes of ADHD

The true cause of ADHD isn't known. However, what is known are the factors that increase the likelihood of a child developing ADHD. Before we look at the possible factors that can cause ADHD in a child, let's have a look at what doesn't cause ADHD.

ADHD isn't caused by eating too much sugar or foods with additives. It's not due to allergies or immunizations; it's not caused by parenting styles, poverty, stress, or even playing video games. If you've ever received unsolicited comments or advice suggesting your child's ADHD was due to any of the above, shake it off. Do not let those without knowledge plant doubts in your thoughts.

ADHD has several risk factors, and each of these increases the likelihood that a child *may* develop ADHD:

- Genes and heredity
- ADHD often runs in families. If a parent has ADHD, there is a 50% chance that the child will have ADHD. If a sibling has ADHD, there is a 30% chance that a child may have ADHD (Bhandari, 2023). A close family member might also increase a child's chance of having ADHD
- Brain anatomy and functioning
- A child who is born prematurely has a higher risk of having ADHD. Similarly, a child with a low birth weight may be at a higher risk of ADHD.
- A child with a frontal lobe head injury
- Pregnancy and prenatal
- A mother who had difficulty with her pregnancy has an increased risk of having a child with ADHD.
- Pregnant women who drink alcohol and consume nicotine through smoking are at an increased risk of having a child with ADHD.
- Exposure to toxins
- It's **very rare**, but there is a risk of a child developing ADHD if they are exposed to lead, pesticides, or PCBs (hazardous artificial chemicals).

Take heart in knowing that, more often than not, you have no control over your child's risk for having ADHD and know that the above factors only increase the chances, but they do not determine them.

Living With ADHD

Living with ADHD can be compared to surfing on a stormy sea that's constantly shifting and changing. Your attention is on the surfboard and the waves, a myriad of thoughts and stimuli. Sometimes, you can surf the waves smoothly and channel your focus exactly where it needs to be. Other times, the waves are erratic and unpredictable, pulling your attention in different and unexpected directions. Ultimately, this makes it hard to maintain a steady course.

Similarly, focusing on a single task or person talking can be compared to being in a room with several televisions on the wall, each on a different channel but on the same volume. With great challenge and effort, you try to focus on one single screen, but your mind is constantly tempted to flick between channels. Focusing with ADHD means you're constantly barraged with equally compelling distractions.

In addition, managing your time and tasks can be likened to being a conductor trying to lead a symphony and then realizing your musicians aren't following your cues. You know how it needs to be done and in what order, but making it all come together to create a harmonious song can be overwhelming.

HOW THE ADHD BRAIN WORKS

Scientists and experts discovered there are differences in the brains of those with ADHD compared to those who don't. Most notably, they discovered deficiencies and were able to relate these deficiencies to symptoms of ADHD.

The most notable difference was in the levels of norepinephrine, a neurotransmitter synthesized by dopamine. Let's break this down quickly into easier terms to understand. Neurotransmitters are chemical signals that travel through the brain and body. Think of them as messengers—they relay information from one place to another. Dopamine and norepinephrine are both neurotransmitters. Dopamine helps the body regulate emotions and is also linked to feelings of reward and pleasure. Norepinephrine plays a role in the body's reaction to stress by helping to regulate alertness, attention, and arousal, and it also impacts sleep patterns, memory, and mood. Low levels of norepinephrine, therefore, impact cognitive, behavioral, and emotional functioning.

Experts also determined deficiencies in these areas of the brain and noted how they relate to ADHD.

- Frontal cortex

  - This area of the brain controls high-level functioning, such as executive function, attention, and organization.

- Limbic system

  - This area sits deeper within the brain and regulates emotions and attention. Deficiencies here can result in poor decision-making, inattention, and hyperactivity.

- Basal ganglia

  - Deficiencies in this area are associated with short-circuiting how the brain communicates and shares information and regulates behavior, emotions, and one's ability to plan, focus, and multitask. This results in being inattentive or impulsive.

- Reticular activating system

  - This area is the major message system, and when a deficiency occurs here, it may cause hyperactivity, impulsivity, or inattention.

These deficiencies relate to lower levels of hormones and neurotransmitters, size, or volume. These deficiencies impact how the brain develops and matures. However, it's important to know that brain size does not affect intelligence. An ADHD child's brain still develops and matures as they grow. When they reach adulthood, these differences are less significant.

An interesting discovery to note is while the frontal cortex might develop and mature slower than a child without ADHD, the motor cortex of the brain matures quicker in ADHD children. This early maturity may explain why an ADHD child feels restless and need to fidget.

This information reveals an important truth. The truth is that ADHD isn't just a phase, learned behavior, or laziness. Instead, ADHD is a disorder that's impacted by how the brain develops, matures, and functions. Ultimately impacting how a child learns, grows, behaves, and matures.

TYPES OF ADHD

Every person is unique and different in their own way; therefore, ADHD cannot be a one-type-fits-all disorder. Instead, ADHD is grouped into three types: inattentive, hyperactive-impulsive, and combined. These groupings are due to the types of symptoms; for example, symptoms that relate to being on the move constantly are grouped as hyperactive, and symptoms related to attention difficulties are grouped in the inattentive type. The table below groups the two main types and their symptoms into their respective tables; however, as you'll note, the third type, combined, includes inattentive and hyperactive-impulsive.

Combined Type

Inattentive Type	Hyperactive-Impulsive Type
• Difficulty paying attention to detail	• Fidgeting, squirming, and difficulty remaining seated
• Struggling to keep to task	• Extremely restless
• Not listening	• Excessive climbing and running at inappropriate times
• Unable to follow instructions (or understand them)	• Overly talkative
• Avoiding tasks that require effort	• Interrupts or blurts out often
• Easily distracted	• Appear to be constantly on the go as if being driven to be active
• Forgetful	• Trouble playing quietly
• Misplacing or losing things needed to complete tasks	• Trouble waiting for their turn
• Difficulty with organization	• Struggles with self-control
• Difficulty remaining focused	

A child with ADHD who displays more symptoms under the inattentive type than the hyperactive-impulsive type is considered predominantly inattentive, and vice versa. A child who displays symptoms across both types, with neither being more dominant than the other, is considered a combined type. It should be noted that preschool children will most commonly be grouped as **hyperactive-impulsive type**.

ADHD in Boys and Girls

Did you know that boys are more likely to be diagnosed with ADHD than girls? According to statistics gathered by the CDC, the number of boys diagnosed with ADHD is more than twice that of girls (2023). This raises questions about why boys are more likely to be diagnosed compared to girls. The answer can be found in the table provided above.

Boys are often the hyperactive-impulsive type, while girls are the inattentive type. Imagine you are a teacher of 20 kids, and there is a girl who often daydreams and always loses her things when doing a class task. Meanwhile, there is a boy who gets up out of his seat constantly and distracts other kids with his constant talking. It's more likely that the girl's daydreaming won't raise a red flag, while the boy's behavior does. The reason for this is that it's easier to notice ADHD in a child whose behavior is disruptive compared to a child whose symptoms are less disruptive.

A second question that's raised is what is the reason for more boys having ADHD compared to girls. The truth is that recent studies and research have discovered that it's not necessarily that boys are more likely to develop ADHD but rather that girls are often misdiagnosed or undiagnosed when it comes to ADHD.

One study found that girls display symptoms such as low self-esteem, anxiety, academic underachievement, requiring extra assistance with their homework, having problems with executive functioning, and struggling to listen (Jones, 2024). Due to girls with ADHD displaying symptoms such as anxiety, low self-esteem, and poor academic performance, a girl is more likely to be diagnosed with anxiety or depression rather than ADHD.

It is worth noting that while there is a bigger difference between girls and boys when it comes to ADHD, these differences become less significant as they grow older. Boys are also more likely to be diagnosed at a young age compared to girls. In addition, siblings of girls with ADHD are at an increased risk for ADHD compared to siblings of boys with ADHD.

ADHD MISCONCEPTIONS

As hinted at throughout this chapter, there are misconceptions surrounding ADHD. This section briefly discusses these misconceptions (or myths).

Myth One: Children With ADHD Cannot Focus on Anything for a Long Time

Most children are diagnosed with ADHD because they have difficulty paying attention at school. ADHD also stands for attention deficit, and many people assume that a child with ADHD cannot focus on anything. However, the truth is that when children find something highly reinforcing and engaging, they prefer this over other tasks and are more likely to pay attention to that task.

In addition, many ADHD children experience hyper-focus—a moment in which they can pay intense attention to something that interests them. Therefore, a child with ADHD *can* focus on tasks when they are engaging and interesting to them.

Myth Two: A Child Doesn't Have ADHD if They Aren't Hyperactive

Many assume that if a child isn't hyperactive, they don't have ADHD. This assumption comes from the "H" in ADHD, which specifically states hyperactivity. However, as mentioned above, there are different types of ADHD. Therefore, a child can have ADHD without being hyperactive.

Some experts will use the term attention-deficit disorder (ADD) to refer to a child who has ADHD but doesn't necessarily have hyperactive symptoms. However, it should be noted that in recent years, these two terms have become synonymous.

Myth Three: Only Boys Have ADHD

While it's true that more boys than girls are diagnosed with ADHD, **not only** boys have ADHD. As mentioned before, boys with ADHD display more disruptive behaviors compared to girls. Girls with ADHD of inattentive or combined type are more likely to be overlooked and remain undiagnosed. ADHD is a neurodevelopmental disorder that affects both boys **and** girls.

Myth Four: ADHD Is a Phase a Child Will Outgrow

Before recent understandings, many believed that ADHD was simply a child being lazy or disruptive on purpose and that when they mature, they will outgrow this behavior. However, as studies and research have discovered, ADHD is, in fact, a developmental disorder that impacts a child's brain. It impacts the size of the brain as well as how the brain develops and matures. Therefore, ADHD is not a phase but a physical disorder.

In addition, a child does not simply outgrow ADHD, nor does it disappear when they grow older. Instead, an ADHD child's symptoms will lessen and become more manageable as they grow older. Their learned techniques, strategies, and skills as they grow up help them manage their ADHD to a point where it is no longer disruptive to their lives.

Myth Five: ADHD Is Caused by Bad Parenting

This myth was already debunked when we discussed the causes of ADHD; however, it is worth repeating. ADHD is caused by differences in the brain, **not** bad parenting. Some people see a child who is impulsive and fidgety and doesn't listen as the result of a lack of discipline on the parent's part. This cannot be further from the truth. These symptoms are the signs of a medical condition and not the result of what a parent or caregiver may or may not have done.

However, a parent changing their parenting style to match that of their ADHD child's needs can make a positive impact on their child's life and help them grow motivated in learning how to cope effectively and manage their symptoms.

Myth Six: ADHD Medication Can Cause a Child to Abuse Substances

Contrary to the belief that ADHD medication is a gateway drug for children to develop a substance use disorder or abuse substances, this isn't the case. ADHD medications are developed to help a child by stimulating their minds, helping them gain focus, reducing impulsivity, and reducing hyperactivity.

Stimulant medications, such as those used for treating ADHD, do not increase nor decrease a child's risk for addiction. Unfortunately, a child with ADHD is at more increased risk of substance abuse compared to other children. This has more to do with the disorder than anything else. This is because the disorder increases impulsivity and poor decision-making. Another reason is that due to the disruptiveness of the disorder, a child who finds a way to curb their symptoms with minimal effort will find that method attractive in reducing their symptoms. Therefore, the medication can feel like a quick fix.

An ADHD child who **doesn't receive treatment**, however, is at an **increased** risk of developing addiction or substance abuse as they try to manage their disorder without the proper help or guidance on how to do this.

Myth Seven: ADHD Medications Change a Child's Personality

Some make assumptions that ADHD medication results in a child becoming moody or zombie-like. These aren't true. However, they are an indication that the dosage or type of medication is wrong for that child and needs adjustment.

ADHD medications are a trial-and-error process. No medication regime for ADHD works for everyone. Instead, the child's dosage and medication are tested and adjusted until a fit is found. For example, a child who becomes zombie-like or very irritated results from a dosage that is likely too high.

In rare cases, the medication can impact a child's mood, even at the lowest dosage. In these cases, alternative treatment options are explored until a treatment regime that works for the child is found.

DIAGNOSING AND TREATING ADHD SYMPTOMS

The *American Psychiatric Association's Diagnostic and Statistical Manual, Fifth Edition* (DSM-5), is the standard criteria that healthcare professionals will use to help diagnose ADHD in a child, adolescent, or adult. The process of diagnosis differs, but several aspects remain consistent throughout.

Observations and Information Gathering

At the appointment with the pediatrician, you're going to be asked a lot of questions. The pediatrician needs to gather as much information as possible so they can make an informed diagnosis. You, your child, the child's teachers, and other caregivers who regularly interact with the child will be asked questions about your child's behavior and the symptoms they are currently experiencing.

Physical and Neurological Examination

The pediatrician will examine your child to obtain a full medical history so they can better understand your child and screen for other potential conditions that may cause the symptoms. If the pediatrician has any concerns that require further examination, he or she might refer you to a specialist or mental health clinic to determine whether there are other conditions or causes of your child's behavior.

Diagnostic Criteria

The pediatrician will consider your child's full medical history and the symptoms being experienced using the criteria below. They will diagnose your child as having ADHD or provide you with a referral to help your child with their current struggles and issues if they aren't related to ADHD.

Criteria: Inattention Type

Symptoms

- Fails to pay close attention to details
- Makes careless mistakes in their schoolwork or other activities
- Have trouble focusing on tasks or activities
- Appears not to listen when being spoken to
- Difficulty following instructions and failure to complete tasks, chores, or activities
- Trouble organizing activities or tasks
- Dislikes, avoids, or is reluctant to do tasks or activities that require mental focus and effort for a long period of time, such as homework
- Loses things that are necessary for their tasks and activities, such as pencils, books, and other school materials
- Easily distracted
- Forgetful in their everyday activities

Criteria

Children **up to 16 years** should have **six or more** symptoms.

Adolescents **aged 17 years and older**, as well as **adults**, should have **five or more** symptoms.

Symptoms have been present for **at least six months, and** their behavior is inappropriate for their **developmental level.**

Criteria: Hyperactivity and Impulsivity

Symptoms	Criteria
• Frequently fidgets with hands or feet, taps hands and feet, or squirms in their seat	Children **up to 16 years** should have **six or more** symptoms.
• Frequently gets up from their seat at inappropriate times (adolescents and adults may experience restlessness)	Adolescents **aged 17 and older** should have **five or more** symptoms.
• Difficulty playing quietly or partaking in leisure activities quietly	
• Often appearing to be driven by some unseen force to be on the go	
• Talks excessively	
• Blurts out the answers to questions before the questions have been completely asked	
• Difficulty waiting their turn	
• Frequently interrupts or intrudes on others	

Symptoms have been present for **at least six months**, to the extent that they have **become disruptive** and **inappropriate** for their developmental level.

The Diagnosis

The pediatrician will use the above guidelines to determine whether the child has ADHD. The pediatrician will also consider whether the **symptoms were experienced in more than one environment**, such as school, home, and social situations, and whether these symptoms have caused impairment in these environments.

If the child does have ADHD, the doctor will categorize their ADHD according to its type.

- Combined type

  - If enough symptoms of inattention, hyperactivity, and impulsivity were present during the past six months

- Inattentive type

  - If enough symptoms of inattention, but not hyperactivity and impulsivity, were present during the past six months

- Hyperactive-impulsive type

  - If enough symptoms of hyperactivity and impulsivity, but not inattention, were present during the past six months

It's important to mention that **symptoms can change over time**. Therefore, the type of ADHD may also change over time. The type is determined by which symptoms are predominantly experienced by your child.

Treatments for ADHD

Once a child is diagnosed with ADHD, the pediatrician will discuss your child's treatment options.

- Medications
- Training for parents
- Behavioral therapy for the child

Medications

Medication is often coupled with therapy. Medications provide short-term treatments to help the child, whereas the combination of therapy helps the child develop the necessary skills and tools to cope with and manage their symptoms.

Two types of medications can be prescribed to your child: stimulant and non-stimulant. The medication brand and composition will determine whether it's fast-acting or released over an extended period.

- Stimulants

    ◦ The most widely used ADHD medication
    ◦ Fast-acting

- Non-stimulants

    ◦ Alternative options since 2003
    ◦ They don't work as fast as stimulants, but they can last up to 24 hours

Children under the age of six will not be prescribed medication to treat their ADHD. Instead, they will be referred to a therapy treatment plan alongside their parents, who will receive training in assisting their child. The main reason for this is that children under the age of six are more susceptible to experiencing side effects from the medication, as well as a possibility that the medication interferes with their normal development.

A child on ADHD medication will need constant monitoring, as it's not as simple as swallowing a pill every day and forgetting about it. There needs to be constant monitoring to gauge whether the medication is helping or whether an adjustment needs to be made to their dosage.

Training for Parents

Parents of ADHD children will be referred to a training program to learn behavioral therapy skills and strategies to help their child succeed in school, at home, and in social situations.

While this training might take time and effort, it is well worth it as it benefits the child and the family. This training will also help parents ensure that the school can provide their child with the right environment and meet their child's needs.

Behavioral Therapies

ADHD children will also participate in behavioral therapies together with their medication. During these therapy sessions, they will learn and develop valuable skills to help them set goals, manage tasks, and learn to manage their impulsive behaviors, among others.

SUMMARY

- ADHD is a **neurodevelopmental disorder**
- There are **three types of ADHD:**

  - Inattentive type
  - Hyperactive-impulsive type
  - Combined type

- **Inattentive symptoms:**

  - Not paying attention to detail
  - Making careless mistakes
  - Difficulty paying attention and keeping on task
  - Appear not to listen when spoken to
  - Difficulty following and understanding instructions
  - Avoid tasks that involve mental focus and effort
  - Easily distracted
  - Forgetful
  - Losing items needed to complete tasks

- **Hyperactive-impulsive symptoms:**

  - Frequent fidgeting and squirming
  - Can't remain seated and gets up at inappropriate times
  - Running or climbing at inappropriate times
  - Trouble playing quietly
  - Talking too much
  - Frequently speaking out of turn or impatient
  - Blurts out answers before questions are completed
  - Constantly on the go

- **Combined symptoms:**

  - Includes symptoms of both inattentive and hyperactive-impulsive type

- **Boys** are commonly diagnosed with **hyperactive-impulsive ADHD.**
- **Girls** are commonly diagnosed with **inattentive ADHD.**

- Girls are often **misdiagnosed or undiagnosed**.
- For a child to be **diagnosed with ADHD**, they have to have **symptoms that have lasted for at least six months.**
- Children **under the age of 16** need to have **six or more symptoms,** whereas **adolescents age 17 and older**, including **adults,** need to display **five or more symptoms.**
- The symptoms need to be **disruptive** to their development.
- ADHD is treated using a **combination** of medication, therapy, and parental training.
- ADHD medication is grouped into **stimulants and non-stimulants.** They work similarly, with the difference being in how fast they start to work and how long they last.

As a parent of an ADHD child, you must have a good understanding of ADHD to effectively understand and utilize parenting strategies created for ADHD children. Understanding ADHD helps you understand what your child is experiencing and why it is difficult for them to do tasks that are easy for other children. An important way you can help your child is by creating a positive environment that helps them thrive. This brings us to the focus of our next chapter.

CHAPTER TWO

CREATING A THRIVING ENVIRONMENT

Creating an environment where a child with ADHD can thrive requires a delicate balance of structure, support, and flexibility. By understanding their unique needs and providing a nurturing space, parents can help their children not just cope with ADHD, but truly flourish.

DR. EDWARD M. HALLOWELL, PSYCHIATRIST AND CO-AUTHOR OF *DRIVEN TO DISTRACTION*

A study from UNSW Sydney found that "housing indoor environmental quality factors such as lighting, acoustic quality, air quality, and thermal comfort were associated with the symptoms and diagnosis of ADHD," highlighting the importance of addressing indoor environmental quality for children with ADHD (Knight, 2023).

The environment plays a crucial role in the development and well-being of any child, but more so for children with ADHD. When your desk is cluttered or messy, you can organize and restructure your environment to fit your needs. You might be able to block out noise or distractions as you work and manage your time effectively so you can get to all your tasks.

This isn't easily achieved for children with ADHD, as their executive functions are lower. They struggle to initiate tasks, use organizational systems to track what they need to do and when they need to do it, recall information from memory to help them complete tasks, and plan and manage their time effectively. They also struggle to adapt to change, control their emotions, monitor themselves, and maintain self-control.

CRAFTING A GOOD ENVIRONMENT

Children with ADHD struggle to establish and maintain structures, routines, and organization. This struggle leads to difficulty managing their time effectively, completing tasks, and creating a sense of order in their lives. By incorporating structure into a child's life, they're developing skills and habits that help them pave the way for successfully completing tasks, achieving goals, and improving their behavior.

A good environment is a structured environment. When your child knows what to expect, when to expect it, how long they have until the next task or activity, and where they need to be, they're more likely to develop greater competence in completing tasks and feel a sense of stability and control in their daily lives.

Creating a good environment that utilizes external structure assists a child's prefrontal cortex, the part of their brain responsible for decision-making, impulsive control, judgment, attention, and executive functioning, in developing, as this area of the brain is underdeveloped in children. These external structures help them hold themselves responsible for their routines and tasks, ultimately teaching them to self-regulate.

Visual Adjustments

Along with creating structure in your home, you can physically craft their environment (bedroom) to fit their needs. For example, using warm lights with dimmers can create a serene environment in their bedroom compared to a bright white light. When needed, they can have the lights on high for crafts and homework, and when they need to unwind and relax, lower light is more beneficial to their needs.

Wall paint plays another important part in how they feel within their environment. A room painted in soft greens, light and medium blues, and muted tones create an environment that promotes focus and concentration, decreases anxiety, and calms the brain. At the same time, bright colors or high-energetic colors can result in increased anxiety and overstimulation and make focusing difficult.

Lavender plants are known for their healing properties and have been used for centuries. You can add a lavender plant to your child's bedroom or other spaces to help promote calm and relaxation.

Implementing Structure

How often has your ADHD child asked what's next on their schedule or what they should be doing or mixed up their schedule and forgot about an important school activity? How often has this led to conflict or outbursts? By implementing the following structures into your lives, you're improving not only your ADHD child's environment but also that of the whole family.

Some reasons for crafting a structured environment are:

- It provides external control for your child with ADHD.
- There are fewer arguments and conflicts, and it improves behavior.
- It helps them build skills and habits to promote independence.
- It helps the whole family develop a routine and structure and doesn't let your ADHD child feel left out.
- It helps build a foundation for success by building their self-esteem, reinforcing positive behavior and habits, and helping them feel good about their successes.

Family Schedule

Post your family's schedule where it can be seen often, such as the fridge, kitchen wall, or living area. The schedule should have a dedicated space for each family member and be color-coded.

This family schedule should include when you, as parents, will be at work and when and where extracurricular activities are, with clear expectations of how long they will be at these activities. The schedule should include eating times, morning routines, and bedtime routines. This allows your ADHD child to return to this schedule and know what's expected of them, which task needs to be initiated next, and how long they're expected to spend on this schedule. It also helps them maintain a routine, hold themselves responsible, and promote independence.

Weekly Meal Planner

Not knowing what to expect can cause a child, especially an ADHD child, to feel overwhelmed and anxious. ADHD can also cause your child to be picky and particular about the foods they eat. Establishing a weekly meal planner helps your child know what they can expect from every meal plan; it also gives you, as a parent, peace of mind to know what to make for lunch and dinner and removes the need for quick decisions regarding meals. Including your child in this planning promotes a sense of control.

Behavioral Modification System

Implementing a system in their environment that promotes and encourages good behavior can help them develop good habits and skills while helping you reinforce positive behaviors. Focus on one to two behavioral modification goals at a time. This ensures you're not overwhelming them and helps them focus on one to two behaviors at a time until this becomes a habit.

For example, if your child has regular outbursts when being talked to, you can set a goal in which they're expected to speak calmly when being spoken to. After achieving this behavior for that day, they can add a star or sticker to their modification board. Once a set amount of stickers has been reached, the child can get a reward. This reward should be something that has a positive influence on them and promotes good behavior.

Chore Chart

Children should help out around the house, but expecting them to initiate and keep track of what chores they need to do won't work. They need visual and structured reminders and charts to help them keep track of what is expected of them.

A chore chart in which they can see a chore marked as complete can help them feel accomplished and promote independence. Chores help children learn to work together and be responsible. It doesn't have to be big chores; start small with them helping you wash dishes or move the washed clothes into the dryer.

Morning and Bedtime Routine

When it comes to establishing a morning and bedtime routine, you need to be consistent. Consistency creates habits and skills and helps your child remain on task. These routines will also lessen conflicts and chaotic mornings or nights as they know what to expect. This will also help their body create a natural sleep and wake cycle.

These routines must be kept even when they are not expected to wake up early, for example, during school breaks. However, keep to the routine, even if you adjust their time schedules. For example, push their bedtime to 30 minutes later but keep to their routine by having them switch off all electronics, brush their teeth, and read a book for 30 minutes. In addition, on days when they don't have school, have them get up, eat, brush their teeth, and get ready for the day.

DECLUTTERING SPACES

An ADHD child's messy bedroom is more than being lazy or disorganized. In fact, this is a symptom of ADHD. More specifically, it's a symptom of their lower levels of executive functioning. Off the top of your head, list the steps you'd take to clean up your messy bedroom. This can look like making the bed, putting the dirty clothes in the laundry hamper, putting clean clothes back in the closet, putting books back on their shelves, and taking dirty dishes to the kitchen. Ask a child without ADHD to clean their room. They'll be able to automatically create a list of things that need to be done and do them. They'll put this toy away, then that one, put a shirt in the hamper, and put a pillow back on the bed.

For a child with ADHD, this is not as automatic or easy. They struggle to do these unconscious tasks we do every day because, to us, these are invisible skills that we do without much thought or effort. For a child with ADHD, it requires a lot of mental effort to start or even complete a task because they do not know what to do, when to do it, or how long it will take them to do a task. They might get stuck sorting out their books or become distracted by a toy, not realizing how much time has passed.

Decluttering the spaces of a child with ADHD helps them develop and form these skills and habits so that when they do need to clean their room, they have a system they can follow, they know that everything has a place and needs to be put back into that place, and they'll be able to prioritize and manage these tasks more effectively, especially when pressed for time. In addition, knowing how to do these tasks and which task follows another helps them to better transition from one to the other, often without putting up much of a fight, and they learn to self-regulate and control their frustration, impulses, and behavior.

When crafting your child's environment, set up a chore chart that focuses more on their needs for specific chores, such as cleaning their room. This chart should have the entire task broken down into smaller tasks so that when they have completed one task, they can move on to the next task. If you're giving instructions, it's best to avoid giving multiple instructions at the same time and instead give them one. Once they've finished that task, give them the next one, and so forth.

For example:

- Saturday Morning: Clean Bedroom

  - Make bed
  - Put dirty clothes in the laundry hamper
  - Put dirty dishes in the kitchen sink
  - Pick up toys from the floor
  - Put books back on the shelf
  - Put pencils, markers, and crayons back in their drawer
  - Prepare backpack for Monday
  - Clean under bed

This gives them a clear idea of what needs to be done to reach the desired goal of a clean bedroom. Being able to mark off each task they've completed helps them remain motivated and encouraged to take on the next task.

Ensure that children's environments meet their needs in terms of organization and management to achieve a clean bedroom. Below are tips on helping your child declutter and keep their space organized.

Tips on Decluttering and Organizing

- **Store or donate unneeded items, including toys, clothes, and books.** Keeping unwanted items in your child's bedroom will result in clutter building up and cause frustration for them. Instead, take a few minutes to sit with your child and remove unwanted items from their space every month. If there are items you want to keep, store them or put them on a shelf; alternatively, donate these items to someone who needs them.
- **Use containers and multipurpose furniture.** A desk with drawers provides a workspace with storage space for school supplies. Use containers to store items per category. Refrain from combining categories, as this can cause confusion and clutter. For example, keep the socks in a separate drawer from their underwear. Keep craft supplies in a separate container from school supplies.
- **Organize by color.** Some items can greatly benefit from being color-coded, especially for children with ADHD. Color-coding their clothes helps them find the item they are looking for easily, compared to causing frustrations as they search for what they want. Books and some toys can benefit from color coding, too. Color-coding books help them find and put books back where they belong.
- **Single location for items.** Having multiple locations for items can cause confusion and frustration for children with ADHD as it doesn't provide them with

a clear and defined place for a specific item. For example, if you keep shoes in a cubby at the front door but also in their bedroom, reduce these locations by moving all their shoes to the front door cubbies. Similarly, all school supplies should be in one place instead of in their bedroom and another area of the house.

- **Have a large trash bin and laundry hamper with a lid in their bedroom.** Teach them to throw trash into the trash bin and dirty clothes into the laundry hamper. You'll have to repeat this often, so have patience and be consistent. With time, they'll develop a habit and understand what things to throw out and that their dirty clothes go into the hamper, not the floor. This helps reduce the possibility of clutter building up in their room as they learn that even these items have places where they belong.

- **Use clear containers and uniform labels on all containers, drawers, and storage items.** Clear containers help your child see exactly what goes into each container and help them find items they are looking for more easily. When using labels, ensure that they are in the same font, and where possible, use pictures to depict what's stored in that container. Use drawer dividers to help your child keep their school supplies organized in their desk drawers.

- **Display achievements and rewards.** Part of turning your child's messy room into a thriving environment is displaying their achievements and awards where they can see them and be reminded that you're proud of them. Many children with special needs may struggle with low self-esteem because they compare themselves to other children or their siblings.

Displaying their achievements and awards shows them you're proud of them and increases their self-esteem. So, be proud and display their improved grade, which went from a C to a B.

- **Designated areas for designated activities.** If possible, divide your child's bedroom into designated areas or create these areas throughout the house. You'll want a **designated homework area** with a desk and chair, either in their room, at the dinner table, or at the kitchen counter. Their supplies should also be easily accessible from these areas. This will help them know that when they are in this area, they need to focus on a specific task; it also keeps these items in this area and prevents them from becoming cluttered in other areas of the house. A **designated distraction-free zone** helps them relax, play, and study. This area should be free from electronics and other items that may be a big distraction to them. Lastly, **create a cozy sanctuary** where they can sit and read a book with minimal distractions. This area can be decorated with their favorite items and will be an area where they can unwind and feel safe.

Managing the Clutter

Every item in your child's room should have a designated location—a place where it belongs. Their favorite toy that they carry around should have a designated area for when they go to school, such as their bed or bedside table. Their backpack should also have a designated spot.

Establish a routine with your child where you spend around 10 minutes tidying their room. During this time, guide them on what they should be doing, helping them when needed, but allow them to do it by themselves. As they grow more confident, you can slowly lessen your involvement in tidying their room. Supervise, remind, and give gentle pushes, but don't do it for them.

Every month, spend a few minutes and help your child purge and sort through the items they no longer need or want. Store what you want to keep and donate the rest. This will decrease the likelihood of clutter building up in their spaces.

Be positive and supportive. Staying organized is harder for children with ADHD; be patient with them and do not grow frustrated or discouraged, as these are effort killers. Look for clues as to where the system needs improvement. If your child is consistently struggling with one aspect, understand why and see how you can adapt and change it to fit their needs better. This will benefit them and you.

ESTABLISHING ROUTINES

Routines create stability, predictability, and a sense of control in your child's life. When they can predict what activity happens next, they are less likely to battle you and make smoother transitions. Routines help them manage their time more effectively, empower them to manage their symptoms, and help them thrive in their routines.

You'll want to establish routines for specific activities and tasks they need to perform daily, such as:

- A morning routine for a smooth start to the day
- A bedtime routine to help them form healthy sleeping habits

- A homework and study routine to aid in their academic performance
- A routine focused on mindfulness and relaxation for when they're feeling overwhelmed or anxious
- A routine focused on exercise and physical activity

You can also set up routines around their extracurriculars; for example, set a routine to help them prepare for swim or soccer practice in which they eat, get dressed, and make sure they have everything they need before you take them.

Visual Tools for Routine Creation

Use visual aids to help your child keep to their routine. Below are tips on incorporating visual tools into your routines to help your child keep to task, transition between tasks, and keep organized.

- **Daily routine schedule.** Have their daily routine posted on a wall with colorful cues for each task and activity, and include visuals and instructions to help them move from one task to the next. For example, block out time for their morning routine on this schedule and provide visual cues to guide them through it, such as getting dressed, eating breakfast, brushing their teeth, putting on their shoes, and grabbing their coat and backpack.
- **Use visual timers.** Help your child understand the concept of time and track their tasks by incorporating visual timers. These timers can help them see what time remains for each activity and nurture time awareness. It also helps them transition from one task to another when needed.

- **Checklists for tasks.** Create checklists for consistent tasks your child needs to perform daily. For example, have a checklist that breaks down their homework routine into meaningful steps that ensure they hand over any important permission slips or communication from the school to you, followed by checking what homework they have for that day and writing down their due dates on their school calendar. Using a checklist for the items they need daily for school can help them ensure their school backpack is checked and ready the night before.
- **Homework planner.** As suggested above, a checklist for their backpack can ensure they stay on top of important school dates. Having a homework planner where your child can write down all their homework, assignments, and test days can help them remember and schedule these items so they aren't forgotten.

Routines should be **flexible**. When you notice your child is overwhelmed, let them take a break and have them complete the task later. Yes, keeping to a routine is important, but your child will have days when they need to take a break or have therapy or medication that interferes with their routine. The routine should match these needs.

Provide your child with **transition cues**. When your child is busy with an activity, gently remind them they have 10 minutes left before they need to do another task. Then, give them another reminder when there are two minutes left and suggest that they pack away their toys or tidy up during those two minutes. This helps them be mentally prepared for the change in activities.

CULTIVATE CONSISTENCY

Consistency allows boundaries and expectations to be set, gives power to your words, and helps your child learn to control their behaviors by being consistent in schedules, routines, rules, discipline patterns, and how you connect emotionally with your child. Children learn through observation, internalization, and repetition. When you're consistent, you cultivate an environment and relationship with your child that makes them feel safe, clearly defines your rules and expectations, and reduces the possibility of tantrums, meltdowns, and other inappropriate behavior.

Inconsistency is harmful as it removes your child's sense of safety and predictability, causes confusion and anxiety, and teaches them that they cannot count on your rules and expectations. Inconsistency causes your child to feel overwhelmed, and to fight these feelings, they solve their problems with undesirable behavior. They may grow aggressive, hostile, complacent, confused, unruly, and passive toward you and other caregivers. Therefore, you must cultivate consistency.

Feeling exhausted, frustrated, and stressed can tempt you to become inconsistent. You grow frustrated when you've repeatedly asked them to do something, and they still haven't done it, so you do it yourself. We are all human, and we all make mistakes. You must be empathetic toward yourself and acknowledge when it's been a difficult day and when you feel like you are not being consistent. But, also remind yourself that consistency is an investment in your child's development and cultivating a stronger relationship, and while you're tempted to be inconsistent right now, your future self will thank you for staying consistent.

Steps for More Consistency

1. Lay down house rules and consequences for breaking these rules.
2. Write down the top three issues you and your partner are experiencing, specifically issues where your children are uncooperative.
3. If your children are old enough, sit down with them and brainstorm solutions. Remember, this isn't about blaming or punishing; it's about problem-solving.
4. Discuss with your partner the consequences you've established and identify where you will need to support each other in enforcing these consequences consistently. You and your partner must be on the same page for this to work.
5. Have a family meeting where you go over the rules and consequences and ensure that every member fully understands what is expected of them and the consequences if they break these rules. Post the rules and consequences so they can easily be seen.
6. Check-in every three months to evaluate how these rules are working, identifying where adjustments need to be made and where additional rules or consequences need to be established.

INVOLVING YOUR KID

Include your child in crafting their thriving environment; this helps them feel in control of the changes happening to their environment and helps them communicate specific needs.

Start small. Even though you might be tempted to jump right in, focus on small things to help your child understand these changes and get used to them.

Do one room at a time. Organization and creating routines and schedules don't happen overnight. They take time, patience, and revision. Take it slow and do one room at a time when organizing and decluttering.

Perfection is not the goal. When your child wants to have an odd structure to their environment, don't fight it. Instead, try to understand why they want a dinosaur in their reading corner. And when things get a bit messy, don't stress. It takes time to build habits and routines.

Assign tasks to them and let them help out. When you're organizing the living room drawers, let them help. When cleaning the cupboards, let them grab a cloth and help you. This is a great bonding activity that teaches them about helping with household chores.

Stick to the lists you make. As difficult as it is sometimes to stick to the lists you create to organize and declutter, stick to them. You are modeling appropriate behavior that your child with ADHD will observe, internalize, and mimic. If they see you keep to the tasks you lay out for yourself, they are more likely to keep to their tasks, too.

30-DAY DECLUTTERING AND ORGANIZATION CHALLENGE

DAY	FOCUS	INSTRUCTIONS
1	Bedroom: The bed	<ul><li>Clear the bed of any items that don't belong.</li><li>Change the sheets.</li><li>Let them pick one toy they can keep on their bed. Any other toys should be stored with their other toys.</li></ul>
2	Bedroom: The desk	<ul><li>Clear out the desk and drawers.</li><li>Organize the drawers with dividers.</li><li>Only store school supplies in the drawers.</li><li>Organize the desk space so they aren't distracted by items on the desk and can see their calendar and schedule with ease.</li></ul>
3	Bedroom: Trash bin	<ul><li>Dedicate a space for a large trash bin. This space should be within reach of where they need it and reduce their habit of keeping trash in their bed, on the floor, or on their desks.</li></ul>
4	Bedroom: Bookshelf	<ul><li>Sort through the books on their bookshelves and determine what you're keeping.</li><li>Let your child decide how they want to organize their books.</li></ul>
5	Bedroom: Reading spot	<ul><li>Create a designated spot near the bookshelf.</li><li>Let your child decide how they want their space to be laid out.</li></ul>
6	Bedroom: Label it	<ul><li>Label everything that needs labeling to help your child know where to put what.</li><li>Let them help you stick these labels or pick the pictures for the labels.</li></ul>

7	Bedroom: Under the bed	• Clear out everything under their bed and find where everything needs to go.
8	Bedroom: Space for tomorrow's outfit	• Help them designate a space in their room or closet where they lay out their clothes for the next day.
9	Bedroom: Seasonal clothes	• Remove off-season clothes from their closet and store them. • Clearly label the containers with the off-season clothes.
10	Bedroom: Clothes categorization	• Sort their clothes by type: shirts, pants, sweatshirts, etc. • Then, sort them by color.
11	Bedroom: Laundry hamper	• Find a designated area for their laundry hamper, where they'll be reminded to put their dirty clothes in.
12	Bedroom: Shoe racks	• Sort through their shoes. • Shoe racks can help organize shoes and make it easier for them to find the ones they're looking for. • Categorize shoes by type.
13	Play area: A home for toys	• Make sure every toy has a place in their play area. • Use containers and bins to keep their toys organized. • Ensure there are clear labels on the containers.
14	Play area: Old toys	• Toss or donate any old toys. • Let them decide what toys they can part with. • Set a limit: for example, only toys that fit can stay, and the rest have to go.

15	Play area: Items to repurpose	• Search through your storage spaces for items to be used in your child's play area—old tablecloths, old bowls, etc.
16	Play area: Stations	• Create stations in their play area dedicated to similar items, such as their toy kitchen, which holds all their kitchen toys—an area where their trains and cars can be played together. • Encourage them to keep these toys in their designated stations.
17	Play area: Storage	• Get creative with where you hide or store items. Study containers can be used as seating areas.
18	Play area: Walls	• To use up empty spaces, they can hang their dress-up items, collectibles, or other items on the wall.
19	Routine and Schedule: Planner	• Teach them how to use their homework planner. • Make sure they write down all their assignments, practice days, and playdates in the planner.
20	Routine and Schedule: Master calendar	• Keep track of every family member's schedule by clearly displaying them on a calendar where everyone can see and be reminded.
21	School: School shelf	• Create a shelf or space where your child places anything they need to bring to school the next day.
22	School: Backpack cleaning	• Clear out the backpack and clean it.
23	School: Backpack organization	• Organize their backpack into different compartments and clearly label them.

24	School: Backpack supplies	• Sort the school supplies according to type—notebooks together, pencils together, and so forth.
25	School: Designated place for backpack	• Create a designated space for everything within the backpack. • Let your child take everything out and put them back in so they learn where and what needs to go.
26	School: Everyday checklist	• Create a checklist of all the things your child needs to take to school every day and attach it to their backpack.
27	School: IEP set up	• If your child has been diagnosed with ADHD, they're entitled by U.S law to IEP. If you haven't enrolled them already, now is the best time to enroll them. • This allows them to maintain additional textbooks for when they forget one at school.
28	School: Achievement space	• Create a designated area to display any awards and achievements. • Display their best work in a commonly seen place.
29	Study area: Create the space	• Create a designated area where they will do homework and study. • If this is in a common area, create a container that contains all the items they'll need for homework or studying.
30	Evaluation and adjustments	• Start from day one, go through the systems you've created, and determine which are working and which need to be adjusted or changed. • Consider evaluating which tasks or activities your child engaged in, enjoyed, and which they struggled with and how you can work toward helping them develop these skills.

CHAPTER THREE

TRANSFORMING CHALLENGES INTO TRIUMPHS
BEHAVIOR MANAGEMENT STRATEGIES

I wish people simply knew that ADHD is so much more than just "being hyper."

S.S.

ADHD isn't just a neurodevelopmental disorder that results in symptoms. Children with ADHD struggle with more than just the symptoms of the disorder; they struggle with how these symptoms impact their behavior and how it makes it more challenging for them to manage their behaviors. Different ADHD symptoms result in different behavioral challenges that can make it difficult for your child to handle their behavior as well as make it challenging for you as a parent to get a handle on these behaviors.

FACING CHALLENGING BEHAVIORS

The behaviors your child may commonly experience can be grouped according to their ADHD type. It is worth noting that even though your child may not be of inattentive type, they may display similar behavioral challenges and vice versa. Therefore, understanding how their ADHD results in these behavioral challenges will help you guide and teach them how to manage their behaviors.

Inattention

An inattentive ADHD child primarily struggles with being distracted, forgetful, and disorganized and may display little to no hyperactivity. These symptoms make them less disruptive but increase the probability that they'll fly under the radar and be misunderstood as insensitive, spacey, and lazy.

The hippocampus is a structure within the brain involved in learning and memory. For a normal child, this area of the brain works similarly to a clerk filing documents. The clerk receives a file, notes where it needs to go, and files it in the correct cabinet for easy retrieval. However, for a child with ADHD, their clerk is carrying a huge load of files, with some papers spilling out, and instead of filing each file in their correct cabinet, they all get dumped in one place, making it harder for the right information to be retrieved later on.

A child with inattentive ADHD might advocate for themselves in the classroom and get a good grade on a homework assignment, but what is overlooked is how they struggled an entire day to do the assignment when it was supposed to take them an hour.

Behavioral Challenges

Below are a few examples of behavioral challenges your child may experience.

Over-The-Top Meltdown

You asked them why they were late for school again, and you were suddenly faced with a full-blown meltdown that didn't match the situation. However, while you might grow frustrated and think they're overreacting, their meltdown is warranted.

Your child had been constantly struggling that morning to get ready and do what they needed to do; they were already frustrated with themselves, and your question just happened to push them over the edge.

Not Responding When Being Spoken To

You asked them a question and watched as their eyes got a far-away look. They didn't respond to you and seemed to ignore you or daydream. This response is not because they are listening. It's because their mind needs time to formulate a response. That far-away look was them focusing on understanding what was asked of them and what the response should be.

Dawdling or Dragging Their Feet

You expected them to have completed a simple task like cleaning their room hours ago, and when you checked in on them, they were still busy at their desk, with the rest of the room still in chaos. They're not being slow intentionally. Their mind struggles to formulate the steps they need to perform to get the desired results of a clean room.

Cannot Follow Simple Instructions

You asked them to grab bananas, bread, and milk and meet you in the frozen food section. After a while, you searched for them and found them standing with only the bananas in hand. It's not that they weren't listening. Their mind struggles to store instructions in their working memory, and their mind needs training to store several instructions at once. That's why it's best to provide one instruction at a time.

Starts Something but Doesn't Finish It

They might start a task, then completely forget about it and start something else, or simply never finish it. For example, you start to do the dishes, but halfway through, you find them looking around the house for something. Their focus can easily be pulled elsewhere, and instead of finishing the task they are busy with, they'll start with what their focus is on, like searching for their water bottle.

Constantly Losing or Forgetting Things

You pick them up after soccer practice, but they reach you without their bag. When prompted, they realize they left it on the field. Similarly, they might lose their pencils nearly daily at school, or they often have to search for their school bag in the school halls. Their clerk (hippocampus) struggles to store information correctly and retrieve it when needed, such as remembering to put their pencil back in their bag.

Strategies for Behavioral Challenges

- Create structured environments, especially at home. This can help them feel secure and safe and reduce the chances of a meltdown because your child does not know what to do or what the repercussions of their actions are.
- Manage your behavior to prevent your behavior from contributing to their meltdown. Don't respond with frustration, anger, or exasperation.

- Advocate for your child at school and with other caregivers. Clearly explain that while their symptoms aren't disruptive, they have certain weaknesses. But be sure to highlight your child's strengths when advocating.
- Remain consistent throughout. This means consistently following through on consequences and sticking to routines.
- Use checklists and visual aids to help them complete tasks. These should remind them what they are expected to do and the steps they need to take to achieve the desired result.
- Involve your child in the strategies you implement to help them manage their symptoms. What works for you or other children won't necessarily work for them.
- Teach them to advocate for themselves. For example, if they need time to formulate their response, teach them to inform the teacher or adult that they need time to think so that the other person knows they did hear them.
- Let them make mistakes; this is part of how they learn and teaches them responsibility.
- Be patient with them and praise and reward them for desirable behavior when they've completed a task or followed several steps. This will keep them motivated to continue trying.

Hyperactivity

Hyperactivity isn't a result of a child not wanting to pay attention or wanting to do the task. Hyperactivity results from their brain struggling to slow their bodies, thoughts, and feelings down so they can sit and be attentive. For a child with hyperactivity ADHD, forcing them to sit still for long periods is insensitive, as they don't have control over their hyperactivity, and they will feel punished, which can increase negative behaviors.

Behavioral Challenges

A hyperactive ADHD child may present with the following behavioral challenges.

Constantly Fidgeting or Squirming

Boredom or frustration can cause them to start fidgeting and squirming, making it increasingly difficult to focus or pay attention. They don't mean to be disruptive, but because their body feels like it's vibrating, they need to work off the excess energy.

Constantly Getting Up

Sitting still is a difficult task for a child with hyperactivity. Try as they may, but their attention span is limited, and frustration can increase their need to move about. Hyperactivity can feel like being poked, pulled at, and pushed by invisible forces. You get to a point where your frustration mounts and you need to take a walk to calm down. For your child, taking a break and running around or climbing is how they clear their frustrations and soothe themselves into being able to sit down and pay attention as best they can.

Difficulty With Instructions

Their mind is overwhelmed by thoughts. All these thoughts are bouncing around in their head at once. When you provide complex instructions, these instructions can get lost, and instead of completing the task, they can only complete a few steps. Break down bigger tasks into smaller tasks, and when you present them with information or instructions, ask them to repeat them back to you.

Forgetful and Easily Distracted

You had them sit down for some quiet time in their room, but when you checked in a few moments later, they were fidgeting with their nightlight. You remind them it's reading time, and they sit back down and start to read. But when you check in, they're playing with their action figures. Their environment constantly stimulates them. If you want them to focus and pay attention, you need to minimize possible distractions to help them hone in on one specific thing or task at a time.

Constantly Fighting Their Routine and Want to Play

Children, especially hyperactive children, need unstructured playtime—a time in which they get to decide how they release their energy without being told what to do or how to do it.

Schools in Finland have increased their playtime and decreased their class time, and they have noted an increase in their children's academic performance and less disruptive classroom behaviors. This is because a child who can play and be a kid is free to explore and be curious, and with this curiosity comes a desire to learn and understand.

Strategies for Behavioral Challenges

- Ensure your child starts their day off with a good, healthy breakfast. Hunger and blood-sugar levels rising and dropping can make a child more hyperactive.
- Allow them to get rid of excess energy before they have to sit and pay attention to their homework.
- Break down homework into smaller chunks. Let them take a three-minute break, during which they can choose to run, jump, or climb. Have them return to the homework once the break is over and repeat.
- Create a boredom box that they can dive into when boredom sets in. This box can be filled with the activities and items that often hold their attention and interest for a while. Remember to change items in this box as their interests change, too.
- Let them spend at least 20 minutes a day doing exercises or physical activities.
- If they're fidgeting with their clothes or a fidget tool while doing their homework, let them be. This is how they cope with their hyperactivity to complete a task.
- Learn about breathing exercises and teach them to your child. Help them practice these breathing exercises when they need to grow aware and understand their body, feelings, behavior, and hyperactivity. This can also help them breathe through moments when they can't get up and need to be patient.
- Praise, reward, and reinforce good behaviors, and empower them to associate desired activities with positivity. Use this to challenge and motivate them. For example, if they can consistently do homework

for five minutes, increase every other focus time by one minute. With time, patience, and consistency, they'll learn to remain focused for longer periods of time.

Impulsivity

Every ADHD child struggles with self-regulation; for some, this is more challenging than others. However, if your child struggles with impulsivity, they cannot practice paying attention until they learn how to manage their impulses so that they know what distractions are and how to problem-solve when they do become distracted.

Behavioral Challenges

Those without ADHD can manage their impulses and realize when they cannot do what their impulse tells them to do because there are consequences to doing this. For example, we know that if we don't do our work, we will get into trouble with our manager, and we might miss an important deadline. A child with ADHD doesn't fully understand how their impulses have consequences; their mind doesn't connect their behavior to the consequences related to it.

- Pulling on ponytails
- Touching people while waiting in line
- Pushing their finger into another person's food
- Hitting their siblings when not being watched
- Lying about what they did
- Calling out answers before the teacher finishes the question or asks for the answer
- Interrupting people while they are speaking

- Struggles with delayed gratification
- Growing aggressive or easily irritated when they are not able to do what they want or when they are expected to wait

Therefore, a child with impulse challenges needs guidance and help in clearly and explicitly understanding how their actions have consequences, how impulse control can be worth it, and whether they **can** indeed do it.

Strategies for Behavioral Challenges

- Be a good role model. Your child needs to see how to do what is expected of them, for example, talking calmly when frustrated.
- Talk through your problem-solving process so your child understands how you do it. For example, let them help with dinner and explain how you're going to do it with fewer ingredients.
- Be **explicit** about the consequences of their behavior and what you expect of them. For example, when they hit their friend, their friend won't want to be friends with them. Don't say they shouldn't hit, but say what they should do instead; for example, when you feel like hitting, use your words and tell them you're upset.
- Minimize distractions. Create a space for them where there is no distraction and they're not near a window or a door. Use this space when they need to focus.
- Be consistent and swift in your follow-through of consequences and praise. Swiftness ensures that they are aware of the behavior that resulted in the praise or consequence. Consistency prevents them from

having unclear or blurred understandings of the consequences of their actions.
- Practice delayed gratification.
- Teach them to use self-talk to help them overcome their impulses. For example, "feet on the ground and hands together" is a mantra they can use when waiting in line and feeling the impulse to touch others.
- Let the punishment fit the crime and let minor misbehaviors slide (pick your battles) so that your interactions aren't focused only on what they need to do or what they are doing wrong.
- Praise them when they are patient and teach them deep breathing exercises to help them remain patient when needed.

Oppositional Defiant Disorder

Oppositional defiant disorder (ODD) is prevalent in around 40% of children with ADHD. Children with ODD present with consistently angry, violent, and disruptive behaviors toward adults or authority figures. ODD is more common in boys, but this levels out once they reach puberty. An older child with ODD is less likely to outgrow it, and it may persist well into adulthood.

ODD children aren't intentional; experts believe their intense behavior is due to intense impulsivity, which leads them to lash out physically and verbally toward those around them.

Behavioral Challenges

Some symptoms of ODD are:

- Blasting the TV or radio early in the morning to wake you up
- Trashing the house due to boredom and then lashing out physically and verbally toward you when you ask them to clean up
- Verbal abuse toward their teachers when given simple orders in class
- Deliberately hurting classmates either verbally or physically to the point of making the classmates cry
- Lashing out at their sibling for the smallest things, such as coughing
- Excessively arguing with parents, caregivers, and teachers
- Refusing to do what they are told
- Blaming others for their behavior and mistakes
- Having a constant angry attitude
- Easily irritated or annoyed by others

Strategies for Behavioral Challenges

As a parent, when your child presents with ODD, you should not take it personally, and neither should you take the treatment of ODD personally. Parent training is the starting point for ODD treatment. This training helps you as a parent learn to calm yourself and respond calmly when your child triggers you. This reduces the possibility of your child lashing out. Unfortunately, ODD children have a radar for when an adult is angry, annoyed, or frustrated, and they will use this to get to you, which is why training helps you manage your responses so that you can manage your child's behavior, too.

Children with ODD will have individual and family therapy sessions in which they learn social skills and cognitive problem-solving and develop tools and strategies to help them manage their ODD symptoms and lessen their disruptive behavior.

As a parent, it's best to be consistent, reinforce desired behaviors, spend quality time with them, remain calm even when triggered, teach them how to manage their emotions, and avoid power struggles and arguments at all costs.

UNDERSTANDING BEHAVIORAL TRIGGERS

Behavioral triggers are the things that cause certain behaviors in your child. Think of how when you're hungry, you can feel irritated and annoyed; similarly, your child is also experiencing triggers that cause them to behave in a certain way.

Unfortunately, there is no set list of triggers to help parents identify what can trigger a child's behavior. Many have speculated and researched possible triggers and have determined the following as the most common triggers:

- Stress
- Inadequate sleep
- Food sensitivities, allergies, and additives
- Overstimulation
- Technology
- Mineral deficiencies
- Mentally strenuous tasks

Suppose common triggers such as these can be understood and managed. As parents, it becomes easier for you to identify triggers outside of these that might result in certain behavioral challenges you're facing with your child.

Stress triggers feelings of feeling overwhelmed, worried, and anxious, making it difficult for their already struggling attention to be placed where it needs to be. Inadequate sleep causes sluggish mental processing and can worsen ADHD symptoms, making it even harder for children to remain focused, complete tasks, or manage their symptoms using their learned strategies.

Foods, on the other hand, can cause a variety of symptoms that can worsen ADHD symptoms. For example, food sensitivity can make a child fussy. A variety of things can cause overstimulation and cause the brain to struggle to process what's going on. Mineral deficiencies may lead to fatigue, decreased mental performance, and concentration issues, among others; ensuring a healthy, balanced diet can reduce a child's ADHD symptoms from worsening due to deficiencies.

An ADHD child who is fully aware of how much they struggle to do a specific task will feel triggered when they don't have the capacity to take on the task but are expected to do it. This is where it's important to ensure that an ADHD child has a break before starting on mentally strenuous tasks.

Become a Detective

Apart from the most common triggers your child may or may not experience, every child has unique triggers that cannot be known unless investigated. As a parent, it becomes your duty to put on your detective's cap, investigate your child's behavioral challenges, and look for patterns and triggers leading to their tantrums and meltdowns.

The goal of your investigation will be to determine what is triggering a specific behavior in your child and how to prevent future outbursts. Let's say your son has been consistent in following his daily schedule. After school, he gets to jump for 15 minutes on the trampoline, eat a sandwich, and then do his homework. But recently, you've noticed that he refuses to start with his homework on some days, and when you gently remind him about it, he has a meltdown. Slowly, this behavior has increased, but it doesn't happen every day.

After some investigating, you discover that in the afternoons, when he has meltdowns and doesn't want to do his homework, it is because he has math homework. He struggles in that class, and he is already feeling insecure. The stress of struggling with homework triggers him to avoid doing it; when he is reminded of it, he feels too overwhelmed, resulting in a meltdown.

When you start investigating your ADHD child's triggers, you'll want to note the following few things.

- **Time:** What time did they have their meltdown, tantrum, or display their challenging behavior?
- **Location:** Note where you were when it happened.
- **People:** Who was there when it happened? For example, adults, teachers, siblings, or friends.
- **Events Before:** What were they doing before the meltdown? Were they busy with an activity they enjoyed? Was something asked or said to them?

- **Biological Needs Met:** Were their biological needs met? Were they possibly hungry, tired, or overstimulated?
- **Emotional Needs Met:** Were their emotional needs being met? Were they feeling insecure, frustrated, or angry, and what was asked of them that might have made it feel like their emotional needs weren't being met? For example, are they insecure about their ability to do math and then being asked to do the homework?

When you are playing detective, remember not to play detective while they're having their tantrum or meltdown, but wait until they have fully calmed down before probing to understand what might have caused it.

With the information you've gathered, make an **assumption** of what the possible trigger is. Some triggers will be easy to spot, while others require trial and error before identifying the right trigger.

With your assumption made, **find a solution** to reduce the impact or the trigger altogether. If your child is triggered by overcrowded places, removing them from that environment can prevent them from being triggered. However, you might not always be able to remove them from the environment, so you'll need to **test different solutions** until you've found one that works for your child and helps them manage their triggers.

It's worth noting that in some cases, your child's triggers may be more medical and be caused by an underlying medical or neurological issue. If you suspect your child's trigger isn't something external but something more internal, seeking professional help can shed some light. For example, you might discover that your child has a vision problem that causes irritability and headaches leading up to meltdowns, or your child is particularly sensitive to harsh white lights and grows aggressive and irritable when his eyes hurt.

Managing Challenging Behaviors

Your child's tantrums and meltdowns may make you feel powerless and hopeless because you've tried different strategies and haven't succeeded. You might feel inclined to believe that tantrums are now part of their behavior and there's little to be done. In truth, a child's tantrum is a learned behavior. A child learns that they can get the things they want through their tantrum.

Managing their behaviors when they are triggered is, therefore, a tricky feat. You want them to understand why you're not allowing them to do or get something, but you might also feel inclined to give in because you can see it's greatly upsetting them.

When you're caught in the moment of their challenging behavior, it's important to prepare yourself to manage it and prevent it from becoming a learned behavior they use to communicate what they need or want.

- **Stay strong, and don't give in.** As tempting as it might be, resist the temptation to end their tantrum by giving in. This teaches your child that their tantrum gets them what they want.
- **Take deep breaths and remain calm.** Responding harshly or emotionally to your child can escalate their tantrum into aggression, which can be verbal or

physical. It's best to keep a cool head and remind yourself that you're modeling the behavior you want them to have.

- **Praise their positive behavior and ignore their negative behavior.** Giving a child who is behaving negatively attention by telling them to stop or reprimanding them is still giving them attention, and it results in their behavior being reinforced because it gets them attention. Instead, ignore them when they start to misbehave and praise them when they're behaving well, and you'll encourage them to continue this positive behavior.
- **Consistency is key, especially with consequences.** Your child knows what the consequences are for their behavior. So be consistent when they misbehave with enforcing those consequences. In addition, when they behave positively, they are rewarded. Always follow through, as consistency will help them clearly understand where the lines are drawn and what is appropriate and what isn't.
- **Don't try to reason during their meltdown. Wait until it's over.** Trying to teach negotiating to your child when they're blowing up, and you are, too, won't work. They won't want to listen to reason or be open to negotiation. Instead, wait until their meltdown is over, and then, with cool and calm heads, negotiate and understand what has led to the meltdown and how it can be remedied.

Remember the following few points to avoid triggering potential misbehavior:

- Do not assume your child knows what is expected of them. Demand change with every situation. In every situation, clearly communicate with them the behavior you expect of them.
- Don't call things out from a distance. Instead, communicate important instructions face-to-face to ensure they are remembered and understood.
- Give transitional warnings. Warn your child 10 minutes before there will be a change in what they are doing, then again in two minutes. This allows them to prepare mentally for the change.
- Avoid a list of instructions or asking too many questions after another. Give simple and small instructions, or ask one question at a time to ensure they aren't becoming overwhelmed and have the time to process and understand.
- Let your child have a choice over their schedule. This makes them feel empowered and encouraged to become more aware of their ability to self-regulate.
- Adjust their environment to fit their needs. If they need to focus, remove anything that can distract them from their task. Pay attention to their physical and emotional needs and ensure those are met.

DISCIPLINING YOUR CHILD

Disciplining a child with ADHD starts with you as a parent. It requires that you shift your mindset and embrace that the traditional disciplining methods that work for children without ADHD won't work for your child with ADHD and that you'll need to adapt and change your discipline methods.

In addition, fostering compassion and understanding toward your child can help you learn how to best discipline them and grow empathetic when they misbehave due to their ADHD.

Consequences Versus Punishment

Discipline is a proactive method for helping your child make decisions about their behavior. It gives your child control of their behavior and decisions by providing a framework that clearly outlines what is expected of them. With discipline, there is an expectation that positive behaviors are rewarded and negative behaviors are subjected to consequences related to that specific behavior or decision.

Punishment, on the other hand, is a reactive disciplining method that takes control away from a child and puts it in the hands of the parent or adult, who then chooses what the consequences should be. This leaves a child confused and uncertain about what is expected of them and what behavior will cause a parent to react negatively.

For consequences to be effective, they need to be proportionate. This means that if your child spills milk, the consequence should be to clean it up, not a timeout. Consequences should enforce positive behaviors through positive attention. In addition, effective consequences include using reward systems and timeouts to encourage positive behaviors and discourage negative ones.

Timeouts

Establish the behaviors that will result in a timeout for your child. Discuss this with them and ensure they understand what behaviors are expected of them and the consequences. Create a timeout space. This space should be free of stimuli and be in a place where you can keep an eye on them.

When they misbehave, do the following to initiate and enforce their timeout:

- Quickly and calmly tell them that timeout is starting and lead them over to their timeout corner or space.
- Remind them that you love them and clearly state how long they will be in time out. Use a timer if necessary.
- Once they've completed their timeout, sit down and talk with them about why they were put into timeout.
- Use positive reinforcement by reminding them of how they could have behaved better and prevented the timeout. This can help them with future decisions to prevent timeouts.

Tips On Disciplining Your Child

- Don't discipline when you're angry.
- Give them a clear warning of the consequences if they do not correct their behavior.
- Let natural consequence take its course. For example, if you warn them they will break their toy if they continue to hit things with it when they do break their toy, the impact will be greater than disciplining them would have.

- Have logical consequences. If they break something when they know they shouldn't have played with it, take their TV time away or keep their allowance to teach them that they need to help pay to replace it.
- Be patient and prepare yourself to try different approaches. **Remember** to try one approach at a time.
- Before reacting to their behavior, ask yourself: **Was my child intentionally making a bad choice, or was it due to their struggle with impulsivity caused by their ADHD?** Remind yourself that ADHD makes it difficult for your child to control their impulses.
- Don't expect too much or set the bar too high. Your child doesn't have to master every skill right now. ADHD impacts your child's ability to do a task consistently, so when your child gets it right one day, they might not the next, and that's okay. It's a learning process.
- Don't yell. Yelling might have an impact on a child without ADHD, but that's not the case with a child with ADHD. Model the behavior you expect from your child.
- Most importantly, have a timeout for yourself. Take time every week to take care of yourself. To ensure your mental and physical needs are being met. Carve out time to enjoy the things that make you happy. When you're relaxed and feeling good, you can model good behavior for your child more easily, and your child is likely to feel that you're calm and relaxed and respond positively to you.

ACTIVITY: MY REWARD SYSTEM

Now will be a great time to put your energy and your child's energy toward some fun crafting by making your child a reward system that can help remind them to behave appropriately and help you as a parent reinforce positive behavior.

With your partner, decide on the top three behaviors you want your child to demonstrate; for older children, you can increase this to include more behaviors (for example, making their bed and speaking calmly when spoken to). Once you've decided on the top three behaviors, decide on an appropriate reward your child can get if they've gathered all the required points. Remember, the reward should be something that incentivizes your child and will encourage them daily.

Decide on the total points they'll need to reach before getting a reward. A good rule of thumb is 30 points. For every day your child manages to demonstrate the behavior you are encouraging in them, they get a sticker. This means they can get up to three stickers a day if they have three behaviors that are being encouraged by the chart. When your child only manages one behavior, they are still motivated to continue working hard, and on a day when they struggled a lot, reaching one point still impacts them and builds their self-esteem.

As parents, you will have to consistently provide points for behaviors that are reached that day. It's good to only award points at the end of the day. This prevents them from behaving well and then misbehaving after they've gotten their reward. Or, make the rewards removable, so once they accomplish a behavior, they get a point, but if they misbehave, they can lose that point. **Be sure** to discuss this clearly with your child so they can fully understand what is expected of them and the consequences.

Time for Crafts

Work with your child to create this reward chart.

1. On a piece of paper, write down the three behaviors you are encouraging your child to develop. For younger children, you'll want to use illustrations or drawings to help remind them of the behavior you're encouraging. For example, a bed drawing equals the behavior of making their bed every morning.
2. Color code each behavior and then find a way in which you'll mark the points on the chart. For example, a red sticker is for one behavior, blue for another, and green for another. Place these colors next to each of the three behaviors to remind you and them.

    a. This is important as the color coding will help you assess what behavior your child finds easier to accomplish and which behavior they are still struggling with. This can help you in creating your next chart once this one has been completed.

3. On a larger piece of paper, draw a big star or treasure chest or paste a picture of the reward in the corner or the middle of the page. Let your child decide where they want it.
4. Create a pathway toward the reward. It can be simple blocks ending at the reward, dots that lead to the treasure,

or randomly placed points on the chart. Let your child decorate the chart as they want.

5. Stick the reward chart and the behavior page (and if you created a separate page with the reward) on a wall where it can be seen daily and serve as a reminder.

6. Explain clearly to your child the purpose of the reward chart and the behaviors you're encouraging in them. Let your child repeat what you've said so you know they understand.

7. Depending on whether you're rewarding right away or at the end of the day, allow your child to stick a sticker or mark a point on their chart when they've accomplished a behavior. This keeps them involved and serves as a reminder for the next day.

8. As soon as your child has reached the total points, let them "cash in" their points for their reward. For example, they can take off the chart and hand it to you in exchange for the toy they were promised as the reward.

9. Remember to praise your child for each point earned and encourage them daily.

10. Once a chart is completed, repeat with a new chart and new reward focused on new behaviors or improving struggling behaviors.

Discipline and managing challenging behaviors can be exhausting and frustrating, but it's important to remind yourself daily that this is an investment in your child's future. Similarly, reward charts help your child make decisions about their behavior, reducing misbehaviors and meltdowns. Together with learning appropriate behaviors and managing their symptoms, children with ADHD need to learn essential life skills to help them succeed in life even when they are faced with struggles.

CHAPTER FOUR

SKILLS FOR SUCCESS
BUILDING ESSENTIAL LIFE CAPABILITIES

 *Kids won't "outgrow" ADHD. They will learn to cope with it and accommodate it with A LOT of hard work on their part and my part.*

H.C.

ADHD doesn't have a cure. Neither will your child simply outgrow it. In fact, your child's future success relies on their ability to learn specific skills that help them manage their symptoms and overcome the daily challenges they face. Possessing these essential skills will help your child reach their full potential and conquer the challenges they face daily, boosting their self-esteem and setting them up for a life where they have the confidence to do whatever they set their mind to without being held back by their symptoms.

Executive functioning skills help your child manage their symptoms and teach them valuable skills that can help them succeed in their future goals. Skills such as time management, organization, impulse control, getting focused, and becoming independent are the skills that will help your child manage their symptoms and be empowered to take on any task.

ESTABLISHING TIME MANAGEMENT SKILLS

Those with ADHD often experience time blindness. **Time blindness** is a term used to describe having a lack of time perception. Research has shown that ADHD affects how the mind perceives time and can result in a child spending more time than necessary on a task because they don't internally experience the passage of time.

For this reason, a child with ADHD needs to have a schedule and routine to help them find structure. However, having an awareness of what needs to happen and when can sometimes still cause time blindness. To reduce the chances that your child spends 30 minutes sharpening their pencil because they lost track of time, using external tools to show the passage of time can help your child perceive time better.

Time blindness can effectively be reduced by using a **digital timer**. Whenever your child needs to do a task, such as homework, set a timer. Teach them that when the timer goes off, they can have a quick break and set it again when they start a new session.

Another way in which you can help your child perceive time better is by using analog clocks throughout their spaces. For example, place a clock in their bathroom, with the time they have for bath time and teeth brushing marked off on the clock. This way, your child can look up and see how much time they have left or whether they need to move on to the next task. In the kitchen, you can have the time for breakfast, lunch, and dinner clearly marked. Every time your child looks at the clock, they can assess when the next meal time is or when they need to move on from eating breakfast to getting dressed.

Using this method throughout their spaces can help your child stay on track with their tasks and reduce the chances that your child experiences time blindness and spends an hour eating breakfast when they should have already been ready for the bus.

Whenever possible, use digital timers for tasks and analog clocks for daily tasks and time perceptions. This is because it's easier to see the passage of time visually when looking at an analog clock and seeing that the hands of time are moving along compared to a digital clock, where it's less visual.

Strategies for Cultivating Time Management Skills

Throughout this guide, the importance of schedules, routines, planners, and calendars has been discussed continuously. This section will further break down these to help your child develop time management skills.

Monthly Calendars and Weekly Schedules

While this strategy takes up some time to set up every week and month, this is a valuable skill that both your child with ADHD and the rest of the family can benefit from.

Spend a few minutes every Sunday drawing up a weekly schedule.

- Mark all deadlines and important appointments in red marker. For example, note your child's due dates for homework assignments and appointments that are different from their normal schedule, such as a dentist appointment.

  ◦ Teach your child that red means an important task or date, and they should pay careful attention to when something is written in red on their schedule.

- Mark tasks and activities that have to be done in orange. For example, they have homework that needs to be done every day, regular therapy sessions, or after-school activities.

  ◦ Help your child understand that orange means a task that must be done that day, preferably within the time stated. This helps them associate certain tasks with a higher priority than others.

- Mark tasks that need to be done within the day or week in green. For example, cleaning their room or other chores.

  ◦ Teach your child that these tasks need to be done during the week, but if they can't do it on Monday, they need to fit it into another day. To ensure effectiveness in time management, mark off an hour every day of the week that your child can dedicate to green priority tasks. If they don't have a task for this time, they can pick a task they enjoy and fill that time slot with that activity.

Plan Proactively

Schedule your child's days and tasks around their attention span. If your child can only keep focused for 10 minutes, don't schedule a task that requires attention for 20 minutes. Instead, break that task up into two smaller tasks, with a five-minute break in between. You can always increase their task times as they learn to become focused for longer periods.

For large homework assignments, break these assignments down into four weeks (where possible). Mark the due date in red, move up a week and mark that date in orange, move up another week and mark it in yellow (or orange), and move up another week and mark it in green. For each of these weeks, let your child mark down two to three days in that week for when they'll work on the assignment. By the time the deadline rolls around, your child will have managed to complete most if not all of the assignment, and the due date approaching won't stress them out.

Prioritization Is Key

Red, orange, yellow, and green have been used above to prioritize tasks, dates, and appointments. Prioritization is a valuable time management skill. For children without ADHD, this can come naturally. There's an awareness that one task needs to be completed earlier than another due to the workload or due date; however, for an ADHD child, this becomes increasingly difficult as they struggle to differentiate when a task is more important than another. Prioritization reduces the chances of your child impulsively focusing on an easier task and delaying an important one.

For school work, provide your child with three colors (red, orange, and green). When they write their homework and assignments in their planners, have them make a circle next to the homework in one of the colors, depending on the task's priority. After school, before your child starts with their homework, sit down with them and look at their planner and the homework they were given. If they prioritized a task incorrectly, ask them why they felt it was more or less important and then help them understand why it needs a different priority.

For example, homework due the next day in class should be in red. Homework due later in the week should be marked in orange, and homework due the following week in green. With continuous practice, your child will learn how to prioritize their tasks more effectively. Even when they struggle to pay attention, they'll develop an awareness of how to manage their time more effectively by completing high-priority tasks first.

Update and Reevaluate Schedules and Calendars

Every day and every week brings new appointments, tasks, assignments, and activities. As soon as something changes, update your child's calendar and weekly schedule. For example, if they have a birthday party next Saturday, update their calendar and weekly schedule.

Pay close attention to your child's ability to maintain focus for a set period of time. Write it down somewhere. At the end of every month, consider whether your child needs to have their focus time extended because they're consistently paying attention for ten minutes or whether you need to reduce their focus time to eight minutes because that has been their average focus time.

Remember, therapy and medication can impact their ability to remain focused. It's important to consider these things, as well as illnesses. If your child has had the flu for a week, it will take time for them to build up their focus again. See how they cope with their usual schedule, then make adjustments if necessary. Be sure to involve your child in changes to their schedule and calendars so that they feel in control of what's happening.

To-Do List Boards

Use a whiteboard and let your child write down the steps they need to perform to complete a task. For example, if they need to clean their room, list everything they need to do to complete that task, such as making their bed, picking up trash and throwing it away, putting their laundry away, cleaning their desk, putting their shoes in their closet, and so forth.

By having your child write these steps down, with your help, they learn the importance of writing down everything they need to do. Then, let your child decide which step they want to start with first, and once they've completed a task, let them strike it through or wipe it out. This helps your child visually see how they're completing bigger tasks by breaking them down into steps.

Decrease Dawdling by Setting Restrictions

Consider the time you asked your child to start with their homework. You left as they were sharpening their pencil to get started, and when you returned ten minutes later, they were still sharpening their pencil. Or you left them downstairs to finish their breakfast while you got dressed, and when you were done, they should have gotten dressed, but they were still eating. This is part of time blindness, and using analog clocks and schedules with structured routines is important to help your child stay on task.

In addition to using analog clocks with the tasks marked clearly on them, you can use time restrictions. Time restrictions help your child understand they only have a set time to complete a task and cannot waste time. This works great for meal times and chores when your child may become fixated or lost in thought while doing a task and use more time than necessary.

Set a clear time restriction for breakfast. For example, breakfast starts at 7:25 a.m. and ends at 7:45 a.m. Teach your child that if they are late, they'll have less time to eat and that when the time is up, they need to start with their next task, or they'll be late. At first, your child might resist, as with many of their routines and tasks, but with time, they'll develop a habit of understanding how much time they should spend eating and when they need to move on to the next task. Similarly, you can set a time restriction on when they need to be at the door to leave for school.

IMPROVING FOCUS AND CONCENTRATION

To improve your child's focus and concentration takes time and hard work. You've already learned the value of crafting an environment to help them remain focused, as well as helping them through their routines, schedules, and step-by-step task lists to remain focused. In addition to these, you can help your child improve their focus and concentration through games, positive self-talk, self-monitoring, active learning, eye contact, and collaborating with your child's teachers and caregivers on how to improve your child's focus in other areas of their life, apart from home.

Let's Play a Game

An ADHD child struggles with starting tasks that require mental effort and that they don't find interesting; helping your child improve their concentration and focus through play can help them develop the skills and necessary focus to do these tasks even when they might struggle.

Simon Says

Simon Says is a classic example of a listen-and-pay-attention game. Include the whole family, or have a one-on-one session with your child. For five to ten minutes, play a round of Simon Says. Give instructions and let your child follow these instructions carefully to show they were listening and paying attention to what you were saying.

For example, "Simon Says… put your hands on your knees." For every instruction, start with "Simon says" and pause briefly to ensure you have your child's attention.

Once your child is efficient in following clear instructions, make it a little harder by doing the opposite of what you instruct them. For example, follow the instructions for the first few rounds, such as putting your hands on your knees after instructing it. Then, for a round or two, do the opposite of your instruction. This teaches your child to listen and not only mimic. For example, after you've said touch your nose, you touch your stomach.

Zap!

ADDitude magazine offers a wonderful method to help your child remain focused when they feel distracted. The goal of this game (or method) is to teach your child that whenever they encounter something that is distracting them, they should point a finger, create a pretend ray gun with their hand, point to the object, and say, "Zap," letting their imagination blow the object away and remove the distraction from their mind.

Statue Freeze

Involve the whole family in this game by having everyone dance or run outside. Have one person be the Statue Maker and yell "Freeze!" randomly. When "freeze" is yelled, everyone should become as still as a statue. Let your child hold this freeze position for 10 seconds and then yell, "Unfreeze!" and have them run or dance again.

The object of this game is to teach your child to remain still for a set period of time. Increase the time your child has to remain as still as a statue over time.

Commentator Game

Teach your child to self-monitor by having them play "commentator." This game aims to teach your child to practice positive self-talk and coach them through the steps of their task. Instruct your child to describe what they are doing as they are doing it and what their next step will be. For example, while pouring cereal for themselves in the morning, they can play the game and say out loud what they're doing: "I'm grabbing my favorite blue bowl from the cupboard. Next, I'll get my favorite cereal out of the cupboard and remember to shut the door. Then, I grab the milk and… carefully pour it. I put the milk back and then grab a spoon."

This game helps them stay on task while helping them remember what the next steps need to be. When they're losing focus or struggling, you can teach them helpful and positive phrases they can say to keep them encouraged, such as: "Oops, I forgot my spoon. That's all right. I'll remember it next time," or "I got distracted when I should have done my homework, but I'm focusing now and after completing this question. I'll only have two more left. I can do this."

Other Games

- Crosswords
- Word search
- Puzzles
- Storytime questions (ask your child questions about the story you just read)

Self-Monitoring and Positive Talk

Children with ADHD can be hard on themselves and often resort to negative self-talk, where they call themselves hurtful and harmful things that negatively impact their self-esteem and self-worth.

Help your child recognize when they're becoming distracted by gently prompting them to remember what they're supposed to be doing when they are distracted. Once they recognize they got distracted, teach them to encourage themselves by giving themselves a pep talk. Similar to the Commentator Game mentioned above. You can print out several phrases for them to use as positive and encouraging phrases.

Maintaining Eye Contact

Maintaining eye contact might make your child uncomfortable, but with practice, they can learn to maintain eye contact with people talking to them. To help your child maintain eye contact and listen when spoken to, have them put down what's in their hands or stop their activity and pay attention to what you're saying by maintaining eye contact. Once you've spoken, ask them to repeat any instructions or information they need to remember to ensure they are listening. This will require a lot of effort, patience, and time, but it will be worth it when your child can listen actively by maintaining eye contact when spoken to.

Active Learning and Collaboration

Learning can be a challenging task for your child. However, learning can become active when your child actively interacts with what they are learning. They can do this by highlighting or underlying important facts, as well as asking questions or asking for clarification when they don't understand something in the classroom. Collaborate with your child's teachers to help them grow confident in asking questions or raising their hand when prompted by the teacher when they need clarification.

A child who actively engages while they learn by seeking clarification and answers to their questions is more likely to retain the information than a child who needs clarification and doesn't seek it. This also helps your children advocate for themselves.

GAINING IMPULSE CONTROL

Children with ADHD often struggle with impulse control. Poor impulse control can look like your child blurting out answers or struggling to wait their turn, climbing on furniture, running into the street without looking, being impatient, struggling to wait for their food to arrive at the table, or having difficulty stopping a task when they are told to. Poor impulse control also results in your child acting out by throwing tantrums, hitting, kicking, pushing, or screaming when they feel strong emotions such as anger or sadness.

As you know, self-monitoring plays a big role in managing our time, focusing, organizing, and controlling our impulses. Therefore, it's important that you help your child develop self-monitoring skills when it comes to their feelings and impulses.

The best way to teach your child to control their impulses is to use reward systems, such as a reward chart (which was discussed in the previous chapter), establish clear house rules, encourage physical activity to fight off the urges, and play games.

The following techniques and games can help your child practice patience and impulse control.

Mind Jar

This is a fantastic tool often used by therapists and counselors to teach children about how their feelings, thoughts, and urges can be chaotic and make it difficult to see things clearly, but with patience and taking deep breaths, they can turn things around and settle those thoughts, feelings, and urges so they can think and see things clearly.

- Use a clear plastic bottle and fill it 3/4 of the way with warm to hot tap water.
- Add food coloring and glitter (try to keep them the same color).

- Add clear glue or glycerin until the water reaches the top of the bottle.
- Replace the lid on the bottle and shake the contents. Check that the glitter settles. It shouldn't be too fast or too slow. If it's too fast, replace some of the liquid with clear glue (or glycerin), and if it's too slow, replace some of the liquid with more hot water.
- If you're worried that your child might try to open the bottle, glue the lid to it.

Let your child shake this jar. Explain to them that when their thoughts are racing, or they're feeling too many emotions at the same time, it can feel like the glitter in this jar—dancing and swirling around. Then, have your child place the bottle down and watch the glitter slowly settle. Explain how when they take a moment to breathe and calm down, they can settle these thoughts or emotions just like the glitter in the bottle that's settling down.

Have your child shake the bottle whenever they feel an impulsive urge, overwhelmed by their feelings, or have racing thoughts, and then have them sit calmly and watch as the glitter settles.

This technique teaches them calmness and helps them practice patience and impulse control. Instead of reacting to what they're feeling or thinking, they take their bottle, shake it, and then calm down before acting.

Model and Practice Patience

A lot of impulsivity comes from being impatient and wanting instant gratification. Start by modeling patient and controlled behavior. Remember, your child is watching what you do and will imitate your behaviors when faced with similar situations. So, instead of growing impatient in the checkout line, model patience by teaching your child how to practice patience.

You can practice patience by using games such as I Spy or Detective. Detective aims to help your child focus their restlessness of waiting into a concentration game. Pick a color, shape, or item and have your child stay beside you, but look around and name all the items they see that match your instructions.

Another way to practice patience, especially if your child struggles with waiting their turn, is playing **Interrupting Clock**. The goal of this game is to teach your child to wait their turn and teach them that when they interrupt, there are consequences. Gather the entire family, set a timer for 60 seconds, and have everyone pick an item that they see, hear, or smell. When the timer is up, let everyone take their turn to say what they saw, heard, or smelled. Whenever there is an interruption, have everyone be quiet for 30 seconds and start again.

ORGANIZATIONAL SKILLS

Organizational skills have been discussed in terms of creating structure, setting up their environment, and decluttering their spaces regularly. However, it's worth repeating that to help your child develop organizational tools. You use color coding, visual tools, decluttering, calendars, checklists, and daily schedules to help them stay on top of their daily activities.

Together with teachers, you can help your child improve their organizational skills within their class setting by collaborating with teachers to provide gentle reminders for your child's needs to write down important dates, assignments, or homework activities in their planner. If your child's handwriting is difficult to read, you can ask the teacher to provide a printed handout of the assignments they were given that day.

In and Out Box

On your child's desk, place two file trays. Clearly label the one IN and the other OUT. Teach your child that when they get a homework assignment or instructions, they can add it to their inbox by either placing the assignment handout in the tray or writing the work down on a page and adding it to the tray. When they've finished a homework assignment, they need to place it in the OUT tray.

This helps your child visually see their progress on homework and keeps them motivated. It also prevents clutter on their desk and prevents homework assignments from getting lost.

LET'S PLAY: TIME DASH

Time Dash is a game that helps your child perceive time better and get them active. The game aims to let your child estimate how long it will take them to do an activity, such as making their bed, solving a puzzle, cleaning the dishes, or any other activity. Set a timer for the time your child has estimated, and let them try to beat that time.

Create a fun scoreboard in which you write down the time your child took to do an activity and let them try to beat this time. The excitement of beating the timer helps your child turn a boring task into a fun one while teaching them time perception.

ADHD can make it difficult for you to communicate with your child and for them to communicate clearly and effectively with you. The following chapter focuses on enhancing the communication between you and your child while helping your child find effective ways to communicate, listen, and understand themselves and others.

CHAPTER FIVE

THE ART OF UNDERSTANDING
MASTERING COMMUNICATION SKILLS

> *It's difficult to instruct children because of their natural inattention; the true mode, of course, is to first make our modes interesting to them.*
>
> JOHN LOCKE

As a parent, it can be difficult and frustrating and sometimes feel like you're at your wit's end trying to maintain healthy communication with your ADHD child. The good news is, like most aspects of ADHD, to create healthy and positive interactions with your child, you need to understand why their ADHD symptoms cause communication barriers and how to help them develop healthy communication skills so they can interact with adults, peers, and siblings efficiently.

As a parent, you'll need to adjust and shift how you communicate with your child. John Locke brings attention to the need for parents to change how they communicate to fit their children's needs. One mode of communication that works for a child without ADHD won't work for a child with ADHD; therefore, the modes of communication need to be changed so that your child finds them interesting and effective in maintaining efficient communication.

COMMUNICATION BARRIERS

Communication barriers are caused by ADHD symptoms, such as the neurological differences in their brain structure and function that result in a child with ADHD having difficulty with communication as their working memory struggles to take in, retain, and recall the information they are receiving can result in misunderstandings, frustration, impatience, and difficulty in putting a coherent sentence together as a response. A child's emotional dysregulation, impulsivity, and inattentiveness affect how they effectively communicate their needs and wants and process the information or questions directed at them.

The impact of ADHD on communication isn't talked about enough, which is surprising considering that many of the ADHD symptoms are directly associated with communication, such as:

- Talking excessively
- Blurting out answers or answering before the questions are completely asked
- Interrupting or intruding on others, talking over them, or impatient in waiting their turn
- Seeming not to listen when being spoken to directly

Understanding that ADHD symptoms impact communication helps you as a parent in seeing communication with your ADHD child in a new light—one where you can interact and strengthen your parent-child bond so you don't feel frustrated when you have to repeat yourself but instead grow in understanding of the best ways in which to communicate with your child. Also, you can find patience in knowing that sometimes you will have to repeat yourself or frequently rephrase requests, but it will all be worth it.

Common communication barriers are:

- **Verbal impulsivity** is a prominent speech difficulty that a child with ADHD experiences. Verbal impulsivity refers to the impulsive behaviors related to your child's speech, such as interrupting, talking over others, being impatient in waiting their turn to speak, and blurting out answers, comments, or thoughts, which can impact relationships negatively. For example, in the classroom, every child is given a turn to tell their classmates what they did that weekend. An ADHD child may interrupt before it's their turn, talk over another classmate, or blurt out their thoughts while another classmate is talking.
- **Inattentive listing.** Maintaining attention and focus during a conversation is vital for effective communication. However, inattentiveness turns this into a significant hurdle for ADHD children. Instead of maintaining focus and retaining what is being said to them, a child grows inattentive and distracted by internal and external factors, resulting in misunderstandings and a lack of hearing important information.

- **Speech disorganization** results from a difficulty in organizational skills, specifically those aimed at communication. When in a conversation, a person without ADHD can structure coherent responses to the questions asked in an orderly or easily understood manner. Children with ADHD struggle with structuring their responses coherently and might jump from one idea to the next without fully expressing either. This leads to peers, parents, teachers, and others finding it difficult to understand them when they talk.

- **Poor working memory** causes an ADHD child to struggle to recall important information about a conversation, making it difficult for them to retain all the necessary information to perform the task required or give a full response. For example, a child without ADHD can retain what is said to them by taking it in, processing it, and then recalling that information when needed to respond or display comprehension during a reading test. However, for an ADHD child, this becomes increasingly difficult as the clerk inside their mind responsible for taking in, organizing, storing, and recalling information is asleep on the job, and vital information is missed. This results in a child displaying forgetfulness when having been told something just a minute ago or having to repeat the same thing several times.

- **Hyperactivity** makes it difficult for them to maintain eye contact and causes them to fidget and grow restless when they listen or speak. It can result in a child speaking quickly and excessively with their words, often jumbling together.

- The above may also impact the tone of a child's voice as they speak. They may increase their volume when impulsive or hyperactive to get the words out before they forget what they are going to say. They might mumble, seeming to purposefully speak softly, or take too long to form a response due to their mind needing time to process the information and formulate a response. Therefore, as a parent, understand that just as ADHD impacts how your child behaves, it also impacts how they speak and listen.

ACTIVE LISTENING

Active listening is a skill that goes beyond just hearing what a person is saying. Instead, it places focus on actively processing what is being said to understand the meaning and intent behind what the person is saying rather than processing to respond. Active listening requires that a child (and adult) be fully present in the conversation, show interest through eye contact, recognize and understand nonverbal cues, ask open-ended questions to encourage continued conversation, reflect on what's said, seek clarification, and withhold judgment or advice.

As a parent, you and your child with ADHD can greatly benefit by practicing active listening. This communication skill positively impacts the key areas of your and your child's life. Active listening helps you better understand and respond to the other person with empathy, improving personal relationships. Within social settings, these skills help your child develop new relationships with their peers.

By actively listening to your child, you help them feel more emotionally supported and heard, improving your parent-child bond. Teaching your child with ADHD to listen actively when spoken to will take effort, patience, and repetition. There might be a few bumps along the way. Still, it's worthwhile to see your child being able to listen, hear, understand, communicate effectively, and develop relationships with their classmates.

Strategies for Improve Listening

Below are a few strategies you can incorporate into your child's structured environment to help them improve their listening skills.

Keep It Simple, Keep It Predictable

As mentioned before, when you give instructions or directions to your child, you should focus on giving them step-by-step instructions. This helps them retain the information they've received more easily and develop the skills necessary to retain more and more information. With step-by-step instructions, it's vital to keep your instructions predictable by using the same words for the same instructions.

Predictability is part of your child's daily routine and schedule. Everything is kept the same, which allows them to feel in control of their day. Consistency and predictability in communication and listening can help your child feel calm and secure and open them up to listening more comprehensively when spoken to, as they aren't distracted or overwhelmed by unstructured routines and environments.

Show and Model

When giving your child instructions or communicating, show them what you expect them to do. If you want them to listen, point to your ears; if you want them to sit quietly, sit quietly and wait for them to mimic. By showing your child what you want them to do, you're modeling appropriate behavior and engaging them in actively listening and paying attention.

Showing your child what you're instructing them to do can also greatly improve their active listening skills and help them comprehend what they're being told more efficiently. For example, if they are helping you in the kitchen, show them how you want them to peel the carrots, including verbal instructions along with your movements. This helps your child understand the instructions more clearly.

Repeat, Rephrase, and Repetition

Get comfortable with repeating yourself, rephrasing complex information into simpler chunks, and asking your child to repeat. Repetition is a wonderful learning technique that helps everyone, especially children with ADHD, retain information better.

Practice patience and calmness when communicating with your child, and grow comfortable knowing you're going to repeat yourself. Whether it is to enunciate what you said more clearly or help your child clarify, remember, it's only about echoing your words but helping your child process what is said to them with their ADHD symptoms often getting in the way the first time.

Whenever you give important information to your child, have them repeat it back to you. This shows they were listening and can prevent you from feeling frustrated when there is a misunderstanding between what you said and what they understood. When your child repeats back to you, it also gives you a chance to notice whether their mind accidentally dropped any important information that needs repeating.

Due to your child's executive functioning deficits, their mind struggles to differentiate between important and unimportant bits of information, and they instead listen to everything. As a result, all that information can get a bit jumbled. That's why it's good that you have your child repeat back to you what you said so you can also guide them on what was important and unimportant of what you said.

Practice Listening

Practice listening every day by incorporating listening activities into your child's schedule. One way to help your child practice listening is by asking them what they are doing, listening to their response, and then asking them what they plan to do next. This helps your child develop communication skills by listening and responding appropriately; it also helps them grow aware of how they listened and whether they need to ask questions about what they should do next.

Reading comprehension has reading time schedules daily. During this time, read a book to your child and then ask them questions about what you read. Give your child ample time to respond, so don't grow impatient as they find their response. Instead, patiently wait (modeling appropriate behavior) until they can form a response.

Sound Bingo is another great way to help your child practice active listening while also helping them maintain focus on a task. Simon Says, and Musical Chairs are other ways to help your child practice listening through movement.

Talking Stick is a great way to involve the whole family in learning active listening. Decorate a stick, or find a toy or object that can be used as a talking stick. Whenever you are gathered, ensure that everyone knows the person with the talking stick must not be interrupted and is free to speak openly. Everyone else is expected to actively listen to the person speaking. When someone has a turn to speak, they should hold their hand up to receive the stick. This method ensures that every person feels safe and heard, and it can teach every person participating the value of actively listening to understand instead of responding.

Encourage note-taking. Your child's thoughts and inattention can lead to them not hearing what is being said. Encouraging your child to take notes helps them write down any questions they have, can help them clear their mind of distracting thoughts by writing those down, and can help them retain more information and spot areas where they have missed information and need clarification or the teacher to repeat.

COMMUNICATING WITH YOUR CHILD

Imagine a busy intersection; even though it's busy, there is order in how the cars obey the traffic lights, and soon, every car gets to go where it needs to go. Now imagine this intersection with the traffic lights flashing like a disco light, causing chaos and gridlock. For a person without ADHD, every car represents information coming into the mind, impulses, class lectures, instructions, and directions. The traffic light represents the mind guiding each of these cars toward where they need to be—class lectures get stored in memory, instructions into working memory to be performed and recalled as necessary, and so forth.

For your child with ADHD, their mind is struggling to operate and direct traffic the way it needs to. Instead, your child has cars going in the wrong direction. Some cars even get forgotten, and there's a sense of overwhelming frustration as they try to regain control.

Therefore, communication with your child needs to be like a main road; a car comes in from a side road, drives down the road, and gets directed to where it needs to go. There's no interchanging of information each other; there's no traffic jam in which a large number of cars need to go in the same direction. Instead, one instruction is taken in, processed, and completed. So, whenever you're talking to your child, giving them instructions, or trying to regain control over their challenging behavior, remember that what you're seeing on the outside results from what they're experiencing on the inside.

Communicating with your child can be challenging. It can leave you frustrated, angry, upset, and overwhelmed, but for you and your child to communicate effectively, there are a few things the two of you and the rest of the family need to consider and practice.

Provide Choices

Children, in general, start to tune out their parents when they feel like they are being talked at rather than being talked to. When you need your child to pay attention and listen, give them a choice. This will allow them to slow down and consider which of the two or three choices they find most appealing. For example, if they need to tidy up their room, give them a choice of which step to do first:

- Make their bed.
- Put their toys in the toy basket.
- Put their laundry into the hamper.

Remain Calm, Talk Soft

Sometimes, you just need to whisper. Children might also tune you out or not pay attention because they are used to you speaking in a certain tone when upset or frustrated. So when you talk, and they don't listen or pay attention, try whispering, which forces them to pay attention to what you are saying.

Other times, you'll feel ready to pull your hair out, scream at the top of your lungs, and just give in because your child is having a meltdown, screaming, or throwing a tantrum. Your reaction fuels them, so adjusting how you approach your child when they're not listening, doing what they're supposed to do, or having a tantrum can go a long way in promoting appropriate behavior.

Let's say your child is throwing a tantrum because they wanted more TV time. They start jumping on the couch, screaming at the top of their lungs, and throwing couch pillows onto the floor. Usually, you'd raise your voice and tell them off for misbehaving and soon grow more frustrated and upset. And at some point, they wear you down, and you give in or bribe them out of frustration.

As mentioned before, this teaches your child that they can manipulate and control you and can get what they want when they throw a tantrum. This, unfortunately, also lets your child feel that you're not to be counted on and can make them feel insecure. However, when your child begins a tantrum, you calmly move away to do something that calms you (but where you can still keep an eye on them), such as reading a magazine, watering your plants, and prepping dinner.

Your calm behavior will freak your child out, but it is for the right reasons. They will be confused by your calm demeanor and come to realize that (1) they cannot control or manipulate you no matter how out of control they feel, and (2) you are the rock that they can count on when they do feel out of control. It won't be easy trying to remain calm. Still, you'll thank the future *you* and be grateful when your child's tantrums decrease. They learn to properly communicate how they're feeling.

As they slowly calm down, let your child know that you're there for them and ready to listen to what they have to say when they are down screaming and crying. But, also be firm enough to tell them their tantrum won't get them anywhere. Model the behavior you want them to display when they feel overwhelmed or frustrated. By remaining calm, you're helping them see what they are supposed to do when they feel out of control, stay calm, and work through those feelings.

Get Creative

Visual and auditory cues are great ways to communicate with your child that it's time for a task to be started or for them to get back onto task. These cues will also be easier for them to pick up on when they are struggling to pay attention to what is being said to them. For example, start playing lullaby music when it's time for your child to start their bedtime routine. This helps them transition to what they need to be doing by giving them a moment to slow down and recall what they need to do next.

HELP YOUR CHILD WITH THEIR SOCIAL SKILLS

It's challenging for children with ADHD to learn social rules and skills. Still, with your help, they can become better listeners, learn to read nonverbal cues, understand facial expressions better, and interact more smoothly with their peers in a group setting.

Be honest with your child about their challenges and the changes they need to make. For example, if your child struggles with impulse control and often hits, don't brush off the behavior. Instead, help your child understand that when they hit a friend, that friend won't want to be friends with them and that when they feel like hitting, they need to practice a calming technique that works for them.

Role-play various social scenarios with your child to help them understand social rules and nonverbal cues. Trade roles often and try to make it as fun as possible. Role-playing helps your child learn to see things from the other person's perspective and helps you guide them on what is appropriate and what isn't.

Have a zero-tolerance policy about hitting, pushing, and yelling. Ensure that your child fully understands this before inviting friends over for a play date. Try to keep play dates to one or two friends at a time (at first). While they are playing, watch them carefully and praise them for good play behavior.

Correct them when their behavior is wrong, or have them experience the consequences of your zero-tolerance policy.

Most importantly, be patient and kind to yourself. You will make mistakes; it's natural, but when you do make mistakes, you must recognize that mistakes were made and make amends. If you lost your temper, admit this and make amends with your child for losing your temper. By doing so, you're teaching your child that it's okay to make mistakes, but it's also important to admit and say sorry when those mistakes are made. You're modeling positive behavior and helping them develop vital skills they can carry into adulthood.

IMPROVING YOUR CHILD'S COMMUNICATION SKILLS

Immerse Your Child in Books

The more books your child reads, the more they grow aware of how to communicate. Especially when the books aim to teach a child the proper way of taking a turn when telling a story or the importance of listening when being spoken to. Books are also a great way for your child to improve their language development and literacy. This can help them understand how to structure responses or answer the teacher when asked what they did that summer.

Secret Code to Help Communication

Create a secret code that lets your child know when they interrupt, get off-topic, or talk excessively. For example, when they are talking and you tap your nose, this signals to them that they've gone off-topic. Have them count on their fingers how many sentences they said so that they can stop and give another child a chance to speak. Similarly, you can tap your chest to signal to them that they've interrupted another person and should apologize and let that person continue talking.

Teach this "secret code" to your child's teachers so they can use them to help your child in the classroom setting. This is all about helping your child recognize when their communication habits are ineffective.

Encourage Them to Ask Questions

A big part of communication is about sharing information and developing relationships. Help your child develop relationships with peers by learning to ask questions and pay attention to the answers to show that they are interested in their peers and what their peer thinks and feel. Questions create an interaction between your child and another person, forcing them to actively listen and use their communication skills to keep the conversation going. Questions are also ways your child can advocate for themselves in class when they miss information, misunderstood instructions, or need a recap.

ACTIVITY: ART THERAPY

Art therapy is a structured way in which a child creates a project that helps them work through their feelings, resolve conflicts, and develop important skills. Through art therapy, your child can build mental flexibility and problem-solving skills and practice their communication skills. Art therapy with others teaches positive social interactions such as sharing space, sharing materials, giving compliments, and even asking for suggestions.

For this activity, your child will create a jungle. This jungle can be filled with flowers, dirt, and leaves, drawn, and as colorful as they want it to be. The aim is to help your child find a creative way to express themselves.

Setting Up

Find a space outside or inside your home where your child can work on their art project. This space should have few visual distractions (so put away all electronics), and ensure that the art supplies are in good condition, easy to access, and washable (especially when paint or markers are used). There's no restriction on what your child can use to make their jungle; it's only the rule that they need to make a jungle with items they've gathered.

Warm-Up Activity

To help your child enter a creative state of mind and release excess energy, have them use small bowls or plastic bags and gather leaves, flowers, dirt, small rocks, and anything else outside in the garden that they want to use for their jungle. Running around and gathering things helps them release that energy and get creativity flowing.

Main Activity

Provide them with a large piece of paper or a paper plate. Provide them with simple and easy-to-follow instructions. For example:

- "Make your own jungle using the things you've gathered outside in the garden."
- "You can use any art supplies you want to help you make your jungle."

Get Them Talking About It

Once your child completes their art project, prompt them to start talking about what they made. You can use the question prompts below to help guide you in getting your child to open up about their artwork.

- Tell me about your jungle.
- Do animals live inside your jungle?
- Is there a story that goes with your jungle?
- What were you feeling while you were making your jungle?
- Does your artwork make you feel happy?
- How did you make your jungle?
- What was the most challenging part of making your jungle?

Praise your child for their effort in making their jungle rather than focusing on the end product. You can comment on your child's positive behavior by mentioning how you're proud of them for following the steps, remaining focused for as long as they did, or continuing even when they felt frustrated. Positively reinforcing your child's efforts in their task encourages them to continue with this behavior and feel accomplished in what they can do.

While communication can be challenging, once you learn the ways in which your child communicates and how best to communicate with them, it becomes less frustrating and more rewarding. You no longer feel like you're always frustrated or have a broken record that keeps repeating the same thing over and over again. Instead, you find the moments in which you and your child can bond and grow in your communication, strengthening your relationship.

Helping your child improve their communication skills will be a stepping stone in helping them foster social skills to help them make friends, interact with peers, and overcome common social challenges.

6 MILLION PARENTS

Alone we can do so little; together we can do so much.

HELEN KELLER

Have you ever stood at the school gates, surrounded by other parents, and felt like you were alone? Perhaps their kids are telling them about their days or showing them a piece of work they're proud of… while yours is racing around the yard or investigating something in the classroom you're fairly sure they shouldn't be. It's a specific example, but you might be familiar with the vibe, if not the exact scenario. You're facing different challenges than most of the other parents you meet, and sometimes it feels very isolating.

But, as we discovered at the beginning of our journey together, it's estimated that 6 million children have been diagnosed with ADHD – and that means there are 6 million other parents who understand exactly what you're going through, many of them also feeling alone at times.

This book is giving you the strategies you need to navigate the challenges presented by ADHD and pave the way for a calmer experience for both you and your child, and now, as your confidence is growing, I'd like to invite you to connect with other parents like you. Simply by leaving a review, you'll remind them that they're not alone on this journey, and that there are other parents out there rooting for them.

By leaving a review of this book on Amazon, you'll point other parents in the direction of this guidance, reminding them that they're part of a solid community of warrior parents.

Reviews help people find the books they're looking for, and in this case, they'll also serve the purpose of making them feel less alone.

Thank you so much for your support. There may have been times that you've needed reminding that there are other parents facing the same challenges you are; you're extending a huge gift to the community by doing this.

Scan the QR code below

CHAPTER SIX

SOCIALLY SAVVY
FOSTERING SOCIAL SKILLS IN ADHD CHILDREN

 *Many boys with social anxiety retreat into a virtual world of online gaming or coding because it is safer and easier than possibly facing rejection or judgment from their similarly aged peers.*

RYAN WEXELBLATT

A large part of social interaction relies on the ability to communicate. Children with ADHD find social interactions challenging, and because of this, a child with ADHD will retreat into online gaming, social media, or other online platforms where their likeliness of being rejected by a fellow peer is lower, and they aren't expected to understand non-verbal cues as effectively.

No child, or person for that matter, wants to be rejected or feel like they don't fit in. Recognizing the social challenges your child faces due to their ADHD symptoms can help you find creative and effective ways to help your child learn, practice, and develop these necessary skills to interact with peers with confidence and competence.

The previous chapter focused on helping your child develop communication skills; this chapter, therefore, focuses on using those communication skills to engage and interact with their peers. This chapter will also focus on recognizing social challenges, helping your child develop social skills, helping them explore friendships, and helping your child deal with bullying.

SOCIAL CHALLENGES

We use our social skills to help us interact and communicate with those around us every day. We use verbal and non-verbal forms of communication to express our thoughts, emotions, and opinions. For a child with ADHD, using these skills in everyday situations becomes a challenge as their ADHD symptoms and deficit in executive functioning can cause a variety of challenges that make it difficult for them to express themselves effectively or even be able to keep their friends because they struggle in understanding the importance of maintaining communication outside of structured environments such as school or sports.

ADHD can affect your child's social skills in the following ways:

- **They have trouble picking up on social cues** as they might not notice how their behavior affects those around them. Your child may interrupt or annoy people because they break social rules.
- **They struggle to maintain friends** because they might be intense or demanding without realizing it.

Your child might be called bossy by teachers or friends during play. Or, your child may have trouble understanding their role in building and sustaining friendships outside of school.

- **They go off-topic** during conversations because they lose track of the topic, forget what they are going to say, or get distracted by unrelated thoughts.

- **They are regarded as being unreliable** due to trouble planning and following through. Your child's difficulties in planning can result in them being viewed as unreliable by their classmates and peers. For example, a friend might have asked your child over to play, but your child forgot. That friend felt disappointed, so the next time, they don't ask your child. When it comes to class projects, your child's struggles with planning may lead to them not being counted on for projects and being left out.

- **They overreact** during social interactions because of their struggles in managing their emotions. It's not uncommon for a child with ADHD to lash out when they are upset or have meltdowns at an age where it's no longer appropriate—growing angry or annoyed when the situation doesn't require such a reaction.

- **They initiate a conversation at inappropriate times.** Similarly to interrupting others or imposing on them at inappropriate times, a child with ADHD may also start conversations with people, not realizing that the social situations and non-verbal cues are telling them now is not the right time. For example, a child may ask a grieving adult at a funeral when they can go outside and play or share their thoughts, such as stating that they are bored or don't want to be there. It's not because they aren't respectful; rather, it's caused by their struggle to recognize what is appropriate and what isn't in certain social situations.

Their struggles look different in every person. However, some of the most common of these struggles are as follows:

- Being bossy or demanding with classmates and peers, especially during play
- Having one-sided conversations in which the other person cannot get a word in or has no interest and cannot contribute to the conversation
- Struggling to interact or engage during unstructured social situations such as recess
- Making friends but struggling to maintain these friendships
- Smothering the new friend they made
- Relating to younger children and adults more easily than to peers
- Struggling to understand how they come across to others during interactions (poor perspective-taking skills)
- Retreating to video games or other online platforms, as this allows them to escape the uncertainty and unpredictability of face-to-face social interactions
- Having difficulty accommodating different perspectives and am not flexible
- Criticizing their peers as being "weird" or "annoying"
- Wanting to befriend the peers they regard as "popular" even though these peers are often less accepting of them, causing them to overlook peers with lower social standings who want to be their friends

- Rarely, if at all, interact with their "friends" outside of school. They might even refer to them as "school friends" as they struggle to understand how to maintain or sustain a friendship outside of school

TEACHING SOCIAL SKILLS

Not being accepted in your peer groups, feeling isolated, different, unlikeable, and alone is a painful experience and can be one of the most painful experiences for a child with ADHD who struggles socially due to the impairments caused by their ADHD. It's for this reason that it's vitally important for a child, especially one with ADHD, to learn social skills so they can form positive connections and relationships with others. Many children with ADHD want to make friends, be liked by their peers, and be part of a larger friend group; what often prevents them from this is not knowing how.

The good news is that you can help your child with ADHD develop these social skills and competencies so that they can feel confident when interacting with their peers and be able to make and maintain friendships.

Below are brief discussions on tips to help your child develop and improve their social skills.

Be Explicit and Direct in Teaching Social Skills

A child with ADHD, whose clerk often sleeps on the job or throws vital information in a corner, making it difficult for your child to remember, store, and recall information, also has difficulty learning from past experiences. Their impulsive nature often leads them to act before they think, which can lead to them displaying inappropriate behavior or misreading social cues. Role-playing is a helpful method in teaching your child positive social skills. Role-playing allows you to teach, model, and practice these positive behaviors. Your child gets to practice their social skills and improve their executive functioning skills.

Create Friendship Opportunities

For younger children, you can set up play dates. During these play dates, you can coach and model positive interactions for your child and help them practice new social skills that you've been teaching them. For older children, this becomes rather complicated. However, try to remain involved and continue to model positive peer interactions.

During middle and high school, it becomes increasingly difficult for children to be accepted by their peer groups. However, having at least one good friend during these years is important to help protect children from the negative effects of feeling alone or isolated from others.

Opportunities can also be created by ensuring your child takes part in extracurricular activities. Ensure that the activity captures their interest, as this will ensure your child is more willing to befriend those in the activity with them. It will also allow your child to practice their social skills and engage in conversations with others who share the same interests as them, making it easier for them to practice the skills you're teaching them.

Collaborate With Teachers and Coaches

Unfortunately, at no fault of their own, your child might be negatively labeled by his peers due to his social struggles.

Getting rid of this negative reputation can be difficult. However, by collaborating with teachers and coaches, you can work toward helping your child dispel this negative reputation and start to make positive changes to help them gain a more positive reputation among their peers.

Dispelling a negative reputation takes time, patience, and effort. As a parent, you'll need to be your child's teacher, friend, and cheerleader as you help them develop the skills they need to grow more competent in their social interactions.

Teach Through Internal Dialogues

Children with ADHD struggle with perspective-taking. In other words, they struggle to understand the thoughts and feelings of the other person, and they often lack awareness of how they come across to others in a social setting. For example, your child might not realize how those around them perceive their angry behavior of frowning and glaring and how it can send the wrong messages about them.

You can help your child build an awareness of the perspectives of others by sharing your internal dialogue to model perspective-taking. This is quite simple: whenever you are out and about, or even when watching a show, you can vocalize your inner dialogue to help your child understand how they come across during social situations and grow aware of the appropriate behaviors. For example, "I'm having cringey thoughts right now because that man is speaking so loudly on their phone in a doctor's office," or, "It was kind of that boy to pick up the man's umbrella when he dropped it. I'm sure the man is grateful for the boy's gesture."

Praise Your Child's Efforts

Positive reinforcement has been consistently mentioned throughout, and for good reason. It works. When teaching your child appropriate social behaviors, praise them for their efforts and hard work in trying and accomplishing. Similarly, correct wrong behavior. Don't stay silent because you're worried about your child's feelings—remember, their peers won't be considering their feelings. Rather, help your child by providing the right encouragement and filling them with confidence so they can feel competent when interacting with their peers.

Help Your Child Understand Cause and Effect

Guide and teach your child how their words and actions have consequences and can cause others to behave or react in a certain way. Help them recognize that different social settings require different responses. For example, they can make a fart joke with their peers, but it might not be appropriate with their school principal. When a child with ADHD start to recognize what their words or actions can cause, they are more likely to pause and consider whether they should continue or not.

Practice Reading the "Room"

Help your child develop situational awareness by teaching them what to do in different situations and how to gauge what behavior is best suited for each situation. For example, at a birthday party, it's polite to say thank you when candy is offered, but at the park, they should not take candy offered to them by a stranger.

Situational awareness is also about helping them grow aware of all the individual aspects of the situation they need to be aware of. For example, when in the parking lot, they need to pay attention to cars that have their reverse lights on and not walk in the middle of the parking path but instead stay to the side to avoid being in the way of cars looking for a parking spot.

Encourage Past Successes

The ADHD brain can sometimes misplace valuable memories, such as a moment in which your child was successful in their social interactions. Help your child boost their confidence in their skills by helping them recall past successes through guided questions to help prompt the memory to the surface, such as "Do you remember how well you handled the situation with Frankie's little sister?" or make use of photos or other items to help them remember how they succeeded socially and had fun. This will remind your child that they are capable and that they've succeeded once and can do it again.

Don't Measure With Family Interactions

Refrain from measuring your child's social competency by how they interact with family. We all interact differently with our immediate family than we do with others. Therefore, when you measure your child's social competency, look at how they interact with peers and classmates. This will give you a more accurate idea of the social challenges your child is experiencing and needs assistance with.

Ask About Their Day

Give your child the opportunity to communicate their thoughts and feelings with you by asking about their day. Due to their social challenges, it can be difficult for them to interact appropriately with others, and a way in which your child can get that interaction and practice their skills is by sharing and talking about their day with you. As your child talks, you can help and guide them on how they can express themselves more socially and appropriately.

Even when they had a play date, and you were watching them, ask them about it. This helps you recognize weaknesses in your child's social skills and can guide you in focusing on one to two behaviors and skills that need correcting and developing.

Assign a Mission and Secret Code

To help your child engage in learning social skills, you can turn it into a secret mission. When your child has a play date or a friend coming over, clearly state two behaviors you want to see from them. These two behaviors are their mission for that day. For example, ask their friend what they want to do and take turns.

Once the mission has been set, it's time to create a secret code that you'll use to help your child remember what their mission is. For example, handing them a juice box can remind them to share or take turns. Saying a code word or touching their shoulder can remind them to engage with their friend and ask what their friend wants to do. This makes it a fun game for your child, keeps them engaged, and helps them develop appropriate social skills. It also reduces the chance of them feeling embarrassed when correcting their behavior in front of friends.

EXPLORING FRIENDSHIPS

To help your child make and maintain friendships, teach them appropriate social skills and then let them put them to practice with a playdate or a friend who is coming over to play. When scheduling these "structured" plays, ensure that your child's biological and environmental needs are met first and that these playdates aren't too long. So, ensure your child isn't tired, they've eaten, and the environment isn't overly crowded or has too many stimuli for your child to process.

Set Up the Mission

Before the playdate or friend comes over, remind your child about what is expected of them regarding their behavior. Then, lay down the two behaviors you want them to display during their playdate.

Supervise, Don't Hover

Your child with ADHD requires supervision because they might need guidance or assistance when their ADHD symptoms get in the way of their playdate. Supervising allows you to observe how your child is doing and recognize areas that still require work, behaviors, or actions that you will praise them for because they did well. But depending on their age, you'll want to supervise without hovering. Therefore, be in the same room or close enough to be able to hear and react quickly when needed.

Set up a secret code that your child can use to communicate to you that they need help when they might be too embarrassed to ask for it in front of their friends or when they're struggling and need your help. For example, asking you for chocolate cookies can be a signal to you that they need advice because they aren't sure how to proceed. So, to help your child, you suggest that your child and their friend engage in a different activity.

Encourage Friendships for Their Value

A child doesn't need to have lots of friends or be part of the "in" crowd. Having one friend is more than enough to help them develop self-confidence, and studies have backed this, too. Encourage your child to develop and maintain friendships with those who provide value to them and to be content with their few friends rather than a bigger group.

As you encourage your child to maintain valuable friendships, have faith that your child will find their way. Eventually, they will learn to get a better handle on things and have a deeper understanding of how friendships work, so while they're struggling now, remain a cheerleader who continues to encourage them.

DEALING WITH BULLYING

Bullying in schools is unfortunately common, and as a parent, it can be heartbreaking to hear your child is being bullied at school. Unfortunately, children with ADHD can be easy targets for bullying. However, it's also possible that a child with ADHD is not the victim but rather the aggressor. This is because symptoms of ADHD can cause a child to become a target or act rude and mean to another child.

Some of the reasons a child with ADHD may be targeted are:

- **Difficulty following social rules and norms.** As mentioned, a child with ADHD can have trouble remembering social rules and norms, which can lead to them not picking up on social cues. For example, an excited girl might not realize that her peers don't want her to intrude on them at that moment. However, she does intrude, which unfortunately gives the peers reason to be mean to her for being "annoying."
- **Impulsivity** can create a lot of problems for a child with ADHD. A child with ADHD may interrupt, overshare, be rude (accidentally), play too rough, grab items, or do or say things without thinking.
- **Difficulty managing emotions** can lead to a child with ADHD having trouble keeping their emotions in check when something small happens, or they get overexcited and become disruptive. A child with ADHD may cry easily or often because they don't know how to soothe their emotions. This can make a child an easy target for bullying.
- **Hyperfocus**, interestingly enough, can be another factor that can cause a child with ADHD to become the target of bullying. When children are hyper-focused, they might repeat the same thing over and over again, keep on one topic for too long, or keep returning to a specific activity that they enjoyed.
- **Low self-esteem**, as with other children, can cause a child with ADHD to be easily picked on because they

have a lack of confidence and won't stand up for themselves when being bullied. A child with ADHD receives a lot more negative feedback at home, school, and in social situations than other children. This leads a child to feel unsure and insecure.

It's important to look out for the warning signs that your child may be the victim of bullying or that your child is unintentionally being a bully to others. Correct bullying behavior immediately and help your child practice constructive ways to express themselves rather than toward another child.

Look out for warning signs of your child being bullied. Bullying isn't always physical; it can be verbal, too. Your child's teacher might not be aware of verbal bullying, and your child may not want to share that they are being bullied because they might feel embarrassed. Some signs to look out for are:

- Unexplained injuries
- Losing their items more frequently than usual or coming home with their items destroyed
- Frequently complaining about feeling ill to avoid going to school
- Trouble sleeping or having frequent nightmares
- Declining grades or a loss in the interest they once had in certain school activities
- Growing more antisocial or avoiding social situations
- Changes in appetite (skipping meals or binge eating)
- Decrease in self-esteem
- Engaging in self-destructive behavior
- Appears anxious, sad, moody, or depressed

Suppose your child is the bully rather than the victim. In that case, you might see the following warning signs that can give you an indication to approach your child about their behavior and ask questions to understand whether your child is perhaps unintentionally being a bully.

- Getting into verbal and even physical fights with others
- Part of a friend group in which others are bullies
- Growing increasingly aggressive
- Frequently being sent to detention or the principal's office
- Blaming others for their problems
- Not accepting responsibility for their words or actions
- Growing increasingly competitive and worried about their reputation (or popularity)
- Have unexplained money or new possessions

Spotting a Bully: Three-Pronged Approach

A child with ADHD may not be aware of when the behaviors or words of others are bullying or whether it's just their peers being mean or rude at that moment. The following approach will help you gauge whether your child is being bullied or not and can help you guide your child on what is considered bullying and what isn't.

Trudy Ludwig suggests you use the three-pronged approach to gauge whether your child is being bullied. Ask your child the following two questions:

- Has a classmate or peer said or done something that hurt you, but you believe they didn't mean to hurt you with what they did or said?
- Has a classmate or peer said or done something that hurt you, and you believe they did mean to hurt you with what they said or did?

    If your child answers "yes" to one or both of these questions, tell them that the classmate or peer was being mean or rude but that their behavior might not necessarily be bullying. However, if your child answers the third question with a "yes," it's more than likely that your child has been bullied.

- Is the same classmate or peer continuing to say or do things that hurt you, even after you've told them to stop or showed that you were hurt by what they did?

Once you've spotted a child who's bullying your child, reach out to your child's teacher and school administration regarding the bullying. Have the principal call the parents of the bully and be prepared to do a follow-up by contacting the bully's parents. When speaking with the bully's parents, let them know you're calling as a gesture of goodwill since you would want to be similarly informed if they complained about your child at school.

The parents of bullies are in the best position to stop bullying behavior, but only if we, as parents, stand up and let the teachers, school, and parents know about the bullying behavior. Therefore, you need to be proactive in addressing bullies.

Coping With Bullying

In this section, you'll find tips to help your child deal with bullying.

- **Believe your child** when they tell you they are being bullied. Teachers aren't as aware of what goes on as children, so if your child tells you they are being bullied, believe them.
- **Have open and honest conversations** about bullying. A child who's experiencing bullying struggles with strong feelings such as shame, embarrassment, and helplessness. Show your child, with your words and actions, that they're not helpless and that help is available both from you and the school.
- **Gather detailed information** about what's happening. Using the information you gather from their teachers and your child, understand whether your child is doing anything (behavioral-wise) that's contributing to the bullying and work toward changing this behavior.
- **Do not tell your child to "just ignore it"** because this advice has been tried and tested and doesn't work. Bullies feed on passivity and perceive a child's passivity as a weakness they can prey on.
- **Encourage** your child to hang out with friends (one or two) so they can avoid being socially isolated. This will also deter the bully, as there is a fear that the friends might call the bully out for their behavior.
- **Encourage** your child to avoid getting involved with the bully on any level. They should not argue or fight with them. Instead, when confronted by the bully,

they should calmly walk away and, if needed, seek
help from others or an adult.

- **Teach assertiveness.** If your child can be assertive,
  they will stand up for themselves and call the bully
  out for their behavior. Being assertive refers to being
  calm and clearly expressing that what is happening is
  making them uncomfortable or hurting them, and
  they want the bully to stop their behavior.

- **Put it into perspective** for your child. Help your child
  understand the possible reasons why a bully might
  bully. For example, the bully might struggle with
  strong feelings of anger or have low self-esteem.
  Putting things into perspective can help your child
  understand why this is happening and that it's not
  their fault.

- **Encourage** your child not to take it personally when
  being bullied, as difficult as this is. When your child
  is being bullied, they should not take it personally or
  overreact, as this fuels the bully's continuing
  behavior. Help your child by teaching breathing
  exercises or ways to regulate their emotions rather
  than respond.

- **Collaborate** with teachers, the school, and parents on
  addressing problem behaviors. Established a unified
  plan in which every person remains informed and
  takes appropriate action.

- **Serious threats need to be reported.** If you suspect
  that there is a serious threat of violence or physical
  harm, reach out to your local police station and
  discuss the problem with them.

- **Monitor for bullying behavior.** A child who
  experiences bullying is more likely to bully others. If
  you notice your bullied child bullying their siblings

or younger children, correct and address this behavior immediately. Help them understand that two wrongs don't make a right.

ROLE-PLAYING ACTIVITY: SOCIAL SKILLS ADVENTURE

You're about to embark on an exciting, supportive, role-playing adventure with your child. This activity is designed to help your child with ADHD build and improve their social skills in a fun and engaging way. You'll be guided through various scenarios to help your child navigate different social interactions and develop better communication skills.

This activity aims to help your child improve their ability to interact socially with others, understand social cues, and respond appropriately in different social situations.

Preparations

You'll want a quiet and comfortable place to play and rewards for positive reinforcement. These rewards can be stickers for their reward chart, a favorite snack, or extra time doing an activity they love.

Scenario Cards

You'll also need scenario cards. These are cards created based on the different scenarios your child struggles with that need improvement. On pieces of paper (of the same size), write down scenarios in terms of the guidelines below:

- Each card should depict a different social situation.
- Use simple, clear language. Pictures can be used where possible.
- Create a reward system for each card. This can be focused on them recognizing social cues, responding appropriately, or even acknowledging where they went wrong. You know your child and the behavior you want to work on.

Examples (adapted from *The Cognitive Coach*, 2021):

- Arriving or leaving school

  - Objectives

    - Saying "hello" or "goodbye"
    - Maintaining eye contact, smiling, and having a confident posture
    - When to shake hands
    - How to greet a teacher
    - How to greet other staff
    - How to greet a friend

- Making a new friend

  - Objectives

    - Greet the new friend appropriately
    - Asking the new friend for their name
    - Asking the new friend what they like
    - Listening to the new friend

- A crying classmate

  - Objectives

    - Recognize when a classmate is upset
    - Asking the classmate if they are all right
    - Listening to the classmate
    - Thinking of ways to help the classmate feel better —according to what is upsetting them

- Group activity with a difficult classmate

  - Objectives

    - Taking turns sharing ideas
    - Allowing each person in the group to speak and share their point of view
    - How to disagree appropriately
    - How to resolve conflicts that may arise

- Birthday party with a classmate who's not well-known

  - Objectives

    - Greeting the birthday child when they're surrounded by other classmates
    - Appropriately wish a child a happy birthday
    - Dealing when things get too loud or busy
    - Managing emotions when things might not go as planned
    - Thanking the friend for being invited
    - Engaging with the other children

- - Being okay when someone else buys the
      same gift

- At a restaurant with friends

  - Objectives

    - Greeting the restaurant staff
    - How to politely order from a waiter
    - Acting appropriately when the food arrives
    - Acting appropriately when the wrong food
      arrives
    - Joining in on a conversation
    - Displaying proper table manners
    - Appropriate behavior when they've finished
      eating, but others aren't

Duration

Practice two to three times a week for 20 to 30 minutes per session.

Age Group

This is suitable for children aged 6 to 12.

Instructions

- Explain the game to your child. Explain that you will
  pretend you're different people, in different places,
  and doing different things. It's an adventure in which
  each of you gets to play an important part.

- Help your child understand that they are in a safe space and can make mistakes because that's how they learn.
- Explain how the rewards will work and what their reward will be. This can help them get engaged and grow interested in the game.
- **Start the game.**

  - Shuffle the scenario cards and let your child choose a card.
  - Using the card selected, set the scene. Describe where you are—a restaurant, a park, a school—and describe what is happening. Introduce them to who they are playing and who you are playing in this scenario.

- **Role-play.**

  - Guide your child by demonstrating the appropriate social responses for the situation.
  - Encourage your child through questions on how they would respond to this situation, what they would do, and how they would respond.
  - Use prompts and guidance when needed.
  - Then, switch roles and let things play out. Help and guide your child where needed.

- **Discuss and provide feedback.**

  - Take a moment to talk about the scenario. Ask your child questions about what they felt, their thoughts, whether they think they did well, and what they can do to improve.

- **Provide praise.**

  - Praise your child for their appropriate responses and behaviors. Praise them when they correctly pick up on a social cue or non-verbal cue and interpret it correctly.

- **Repeat.**

  - Keep things lively and engaged by jumping into another scenario until 20 to 30 minutes have passed.

- **Give rewards.**

  - Once the session is completed, praise your child with the rewards you discussed beforehand to help enforce their positive behavior and encourage them to continue this behavior.

Helpful Tips

- Keep the scenarios age-appropriate and relevant to the situations that your child struggles with.
- Adapt scenarios where your child gets one area right but struggles with another. Changing the approach might help them understand where they keep missing information.
- Be patient and keep the atmosphere light and fun. Your child will fight you, struggle, and might grow discouraged when they get it wrong. But remain consistent, calm, and patient, and with time, your child will find the exercise worth it.

- Involve your child by allowing them to suggest scenarios of their own to role-play.

Social skills are the tools we use to help us connect to those around us. Helping your child develop and improve their social skills empowers them to grow and connect to those around them and build confidence and self-esteem even when they make mistakes or struggle. Together with developing social and communication skills, your child needs to build emotional fortitude to help them grow resilient and confident in who they are.

CHAPTER SEVEN

RESILIENCE RISING
STRENGTHENING EMOTIONAL FORTITUDE

> *Sometimes, the working memory impairments of ADHD allow a momentary emotion to become too strong; the person is flooded with one emotion and unable to attend to other emotions, facts, and memories relevant to that immediate situation. At other times, the working memory impairments of ADHD leave the person with insufficient sensitivity to the importance of a particular emotion because he or she hasn't kept other relevant information sufficient in mind or factored it into his or her assessment of the situation.*

THOMAS E. BROWN

Emotional regulation is the ability to understand, label, and process our emotions. It's understanding why we are feeling the emotions we are feeling, how to work through these emotions, and how to express them constructively. On the contrary, emotional dysregulation refers to the inability to understand, label, and process emotions constructively and appropriately.

A child without ADHD will seek comfort in their favorite toy when upset and use it to soothe themselves. They've used executive functioning to problem-solve the situation, recalled that their favorite toy makes them happy, and thus, sought it out to help them. However, children with ADHD have a deficit in their executive functioning, and their working memory is impaired. Because of this, they become overwhelmed by the emotions they are experiencing and struggle to problem-solve and process those emotions effectively. This impairment leads to a child with ADHD either being flooded by strong emotions and unable to let go of them or becoming insensitive to the emotions they feel strongly and shutting them down.

Helping your child develop emotional regulation will aid them in becoming resilient. They will be able to constructively process their emotions and work through them, practice control over them, and appropriately express them. Emotional regulation will put control back into your child's hands when it comes to experiencing strong emotions.

UNDERSTAND THE EMOTIONAL ASPECTS OF ADHD

Every child experiences the same range of emotions, whether they have ADHD or not. The key difference comes in how these emotions are processed. Because children with ADHD often struggle with impulse control, they have difficulty comprehending and communicating how they feel, which leads to struggles in their relationships with others and their emotional well-being.

This dysregulation of emotions is expressed as tantrums and angry overloads. These are both the result of a child bottling up their frustrations and strong emotions and struggling with a low-stress tolerance that makes it particularly difficult to handle any more stimulation.

During these states, a child with ADHD may completely shut down in an attempt to no longer feel overwhelmed or feel like they aren't in control of themselves. ADHD impacts a child's emotional regulation in the following ways:

- **Impulsivity** directly contributes to a child's emotional dysregulation. Impulsivity can lead a child to say inappropriate things or make careless choices that unintentionally hurt their feelings or damage their relationships with others. It can also bring about strong negative feelings that further impact their emotions.
- **The inability to delay reactions** can cause a child with ADHD to react instantly to small annoyances without self-monitoring, resulting in them lashing out rather than taking a step back. These knee-jerk reactions result in a child needing to repair the relationship once their impulse has settled.
- **Experience negative emotions intensely**. ADHD impacts how a child processes a situation, and instead of understanding the situation as a whole, they can experience a setback or criticism as a personal attack that feels intensely painful to them. This sensitivity reduces their ability to be resilient in their emotions, especially when they work hard to manage their symptoms, control their impulses, and experience negative feedback.

- **Avoidance** of situations, others, or even certain emotions can be a maladaptive coping mechanism a child uses to deal with their emotions. A child may also shut down as a way of coping. However, not processing emotions can negatively impact a child's emotional well-being.

- **Overwhelming and lasting emotions.** A child with ADHD may feel certain emotions more strongly than others and become overwhelmed by them. This results in them having a tantrum or meltdown as a way of expressing the emotions that they feel. They might even hold onto an emotion longer because they struggle to use their executive functioning to understand and process their feeling.

- **Inability to communicate and express themselves clearly.** Children can struggle to communicate or express their emotions due to their diminished capabilities to communicate efficiently or have the social skills to express themselves in a way that makes them feel understood. For example, a child who doesn't know how to express anger might scream or hit. A child who feels overwhelmed, tired, or hungry might cry or have a tantrum. This can make it difficult for others to understand their child's needs or how to help them.

EMOTIONAL REGULATION

As mentioned, emotional dysregulation is the decreased ability to manage and regulate emotions and reactions effectively. A child with ADHD may display the following emotional dysregulation:

- They struggle to manage their anger and become easily frustrated.
- They have rapid mood swings. Experience intense and sudden changes in moods without an apparent trigger.
- They overreact by displaying an excessive emotional response to a small or insignificant event.
- They struggle to calm down after being upset because their emotions continue to escalate rather than decrease over time.
- They react impulsively to their emotions without considering the consequences.
- They experience suicidal thoughts or engage in self-harm as a way of coping with overwhelming emotions.
- They have difficulty maintaining relationships due to impulsivity, emotional dysregulation, and trust issues.
- They have difficulty in academic settings due to struggling with managing emotions such as stress and anxiety.

Developing Emotional Regulation

Teaching a child with ADHD emotional regulation requires a different approach compared to that of a child without ADHD. This is because a child without ADHD doesn't struggle with cognitive effort tasks because they can tap into their executive functioning. A child without ADHD can be taught to "down-regulate" their negative emotions. For a child with ADHD, they need to learn to "up-regulate" positive emotions as this is easier and requires less cognitive effort.

The three top ways you can help your child learn emotional regulation are compassion, gratitude, and pride.

Compassion helps a child overcome feelings of anxiety, avoidance, and procrastination by promoting empathy, teamwork, and cooperation. You can teach your child compassion by helping them learn to work in a team. When you as a family have a task to do, make it a team effort. For example, when the leaves need raking, make it a team effort by having every family member play an important part in completing the task. You can also promote teamwork by having everyone wear the same colors when going to the park. This helps your child feel part of something greater than just themselves and helps them share in the goals, interests, and achievements of others.

Self-compassion is a critical skill for a child to learn. It helps them accept their mistakes and show compassion and love toward themselves, especially when they know they have to work harder at certain things. Self-compassion can help your child grow in understanding of themselves and reduce the impact of corrective feedback they constantly receive, which can make them feel guilt and shame.

Gratitude can help your child rescue themselves from emotional overreactions and build delayed gratification, which can promote better impulse control. Help your child cultivate gratitude by teaching them that when they show thankfulness for the things they have, they can focus on what's positive rather than negative.

Help your child develop gratitude by creating a support tree and gratitude jar. Let them decorate a tree on a large piece of paper. For the branches of this tree, they write down the names of the people in their lives who support them and care and love for them. Teach them that whenever they feel lonely or emotionally overwhelmed, they can remind themselves of everyone in their life who cares for and supports them. On the other hand, a gratitude jar is filled with pieces of paper on which your child writes what they are grateful for each day. When they need help focusing on the good, they can read what they've written and place it in the jar.

Lastly, **building pride** is a goal-directed method that promotes self-control, effort, and resilience. When children feel proud, they feel motivated to work harder, continue working on themselves, and strive for better. This also allows your child to feel like they are part of something valuable and important to them. Help your child build pride by letting them be an expert in something they are interested in, such as video games, insects, space, or anything else they are interested in. Ask them questions and let them be part of making "expert" decisions when it comes to their "field of expertise."

Another way you can help your child build pride is by entrusting them to do an important job. Even though you can do it in half the time and half the mess, let your child do it. It allows your child to feel like they are contributing toward the family in a meaningful way.

Promoting positive emotions can help balance out the impact of negative emotions; therefore, by helping your child up their positive emotions, you're helping them understand that even though they might struggle and might have difficulties in certain areas, they can feel good and do well. You've already been promoting positive regulation by providing your child with structure, routine, communication, and social skills development and helping them grow in understanding of themselves.

MINDFULNESS

Mindfulness is another wonderful way to help your child learn emotional regulation by teaching them to take a moment to grow calm, take a deep breath, and do a soothing activity. These activities not only help your child with ADHD, but they can help the whole family practice both mental and emotional regulation.

One study focused on teaching children the benefits of mindfulness found positive results in children with ADHD. The study handed each child stickers and told them to hand stickers out to others in the group, including those they don't know or don't like. However, the children handed stickers to their friends. Then, they engaged the children in practicing mindfulness; this time, the children handed out stickers to all the other children, too, even those they didn't like or didn't know. This study proved that a few minutes of mindfulness can increase a child's compassion toward others.

According to the research conducted by Santonastaso et al. (2020), children who participated in a few minutes of mindfulness-oriented meditation (MOM) three times a week for a period of eight weeks were able to gradually increase their attention span up to 30 minutes, where before it was averaged around six minutes.

Mindfulness, therefore, has great benefits for your child, as it not only helps them learn to calm and soothe their emotions but also helps them grow in compassion toward themselves and others and increases their attention span. Here are four activities to help your child practice more mindfulness:

- **Mindful coloring.** Let your child pick their favorite tool for coloring. This can be pens, crayons, markers, pencils, or even paint. Provide them with a clean piece of paper and encourage them to notice how it feels to move across the paper. Let them doodle, draw patterns, repeat shapes, or create any artwork they want to make. Allow them to choose the most comfortable position to color in, even if they want to color upside-down.
- **Tightrope maze walking.** Use a stick to draw in the sand or chalk to draw on the sidewalk or any other outside area and draw curvy snake-like shapes. You can draw a spiderweb, big swirl, or twisty lines. For indoors, you can use masking tape on the carpet to create these lines. Then, have your child walk these lines as if they are walking a tightrope. Have them do it slowly, focused, and controlled by walking heel-to-toe from end to end. Encourage them to keep going and be careful around the lava around them as they walk as if they are on a tightrope.
- **Breathe reminder.** Life can get busy for your child at times, and they can forget to slow down and breathe. Create a reminder by putting up a page with the words "breathe" on it to help your child remember to take a moment and breathe in deeply and then slowly release it. You can also use objects in the home to serve as reminders, such as a doorknob.
- **Gardening digging.** Let your child go out and dig in the garden if they struggle with remaining seated for a mindfulness activity. Let them help you dig up

weeds in the garden or create a bee or butterfly garden. Alternatively, have them create their own garden in a large pot. The activity of digging and creating will soothe them.

DEALING WITH STRESS

Those without ADHD handle and experience stress differently than those who have ADHD. When we experience something that causes stress, our body releases a chemical called cortisol, which helps our body prepare for either fight or flight. In short bursts, stress helps us get inspired, remain motivated, and continue on a task. However, when we experience prolonged stress, it starts to impact our mental health, and we might experience physical symptoms because of it.

Stress impairs our executive functioning. It diminishes our working memory, impulse control, mental flexibility, and coping skills. Therefore, if stress impacts us in this manner, how much more does it impact a child with ADHD who already has a deficit in their executive functioning?

Researchers have found that adults with ADHD have higher levels of cortisol when experiencing stress compared to those without ADHD (Schultz, 2023). This leads us to believe that children with ADHD experience stress more intensely than children without ADHD.

Children experience stress due to home situations, peer pressure, pressure from parents and society, and the pressure they place upon themselves. Academic achievement can also lead to a child experiencing stress. Because children with ADHD already struggle with executive functioning, when they are faced with a stressor that can further impair their executive functioning, they have a great struggle in coping with stress. Helping your child learn how to use their skills and the tools they've been taught to cope with stress can greatly benefit your child's well-being and help you and the rest of the family grow more aware of developing healthy coping strategies for stress.

Everyone experiences stress differently. However, some common signs can help you notice when your child may be experiencing overwhelming stress.

- **They are displaying irritability and anger.** A child who struggles to use words to describe how they feel will have their feelings bubble over into a bad mood. They may be more short-tempered or argumentative than they normally are.
- **There is a change in their behavior.** A child whose behavior changes suddenly can be a sign that the child is experiencing high stress levels. For example, a child who used to be a great listener might suddenly act out.
- **Difficulty sleeping.** High cortisol levels can make sleeping difficult, as this hormone is used to keep you alert and awake. If your child complains about feeling tired all the time, sleeping more than usual, or having trouble falling or staying asleep at night, they possibly experience high stress levels.
- **They are neglecting their chores and responsibilities.** Constant (long-term) stress can make it difficult for children to do the tasks they are supposed to do. As their stress increases, they might

forget homework more frequently, forget to do their chores, and procrastinate more than usual.

- **Changes in their eating patterns.** Stress can cause a child to eat more than usual or less. Cortisol impacts the digestive system, and because of this, it impacts your child's appetite.
- **They are frequently complaining about feeling sick.** Stress can present as physical symptoms such as headaches, stomachaches, and feeling ill, but it can also manifest as not being able to explain what's wrong. If you notice your child complaining more frequently about feeling ill or regularly visiting the school nurse's office, your child may feel overwhelmed by stress.

Coping Strategies

Some of the common coping strategies for dealing with stress are:

- Eating healthy, balanced meals
- Getting adequate sleep
- Being active by exercising daily
- Spending time outside in nature
- Make time to do fun things, or take time to be quiet
- Assessing the causes of the stress and dealing with it

These strategies can help your child deal with stress by keeping their body and mind active. A child with ADHD needs to learn how to ground themselves during stressful situations so they can move forward instead of having it hold them back.

Step Back and Assess

When a child with ADHD feels stressed, they struggle to see the full picture. By helping your child take a step back and assess the situation from afar, they can be reminded that this is only a small obstacle and that they don't need everything done at once.

Teach your child to recognize when they are stressed and help them step back and look at the bigger picture. This can be done by teaching your child that this obstacle is only one picture in their book of life and that they should look at the other pictures, too. Remind them of other obstacles they successfully overcame and how far they have come. Then, help them problem-solve how they can deal with this obstacle.

Remaining Present: Dragon Breathing

Stress can cause a child to forget to breathe deeply, reducing the oxygen in their brain and making it harder for them to see things clearly or problem-solve. There are a number of breathing exercises available to your child. However, for this one, we're focusing on "dragon breathing," as it can be more engaging and fun for a child with ADHD.

Whenever you notice your child feeling stressed and needing to see the bigger picture, encourage them to take a deep breath that fills their belly and then blow it out like a dragon blowing fire. Let them imagine the stress being burned away by their dragon breath. Have them do this until they feel calm and more willing to find solutions.

Find the Cause: Inspector Stress

When something unforeseen happens and becomes a cause of stress, your child with ADHD can feel like their world is crashing down around them. You can help your child let go of this tunnel vision and see the bigger picture by engaging them in attention-catching questions.

Instruct your child to be an Inspector with you, looking for clues as to why they are feeling the way they are. Then, ask them questions to help ground them, think objectively, and help them problem-solve. Ask questions such as:

- Where are your feet?
- Can you wiggle your toes? Could you show me?
- Now, let's inspect what you were doing. Can you tell me what made you feel upset (or angry)?
- Do you think that we can work together to find a solution?
- What do you think we can do to fix this?

The aim is to help your child look at things objectively, not see themselves in stressful situations, and problem-solve without feeling overwhelmed because they can't see the solution right away.

ACHIEVING EMOTIONAL RESILIENCE

Emotional resilience is not the ability to not be affected by struggles, challenges, and obstacles faced but the ability to power through them. It's the ability to bounce back when encountering a setback, adapt to the situation, and learn from it.

Helping your child develop emotional resilience will help them grow in confidence, competence, self-belief, motivation, and dignity. Emotional resilience will help your child grow in awareness of themselves and understanding that they'll face struggles and obstacles but can overcome them and grow from them rather than be held back by them.

A child or person who has emotional resilience has the following traits:

- Understanding what they feel and why they feel that way
- Trusting in the process and won't give up, even when they struggle or have setbacks
- Facing their struggles head-on rather than avoiding them
- Displaying optimism because they understand that situations change and that having a positive outlook is better than viewing things negatively
- Being strong but know that they sometimes need the help of friends and family
- Having a good sense of humor and laugh because it's good to look on the bright side and find humor in a difficult situation
- Seeing the bigger picture and changing their perspective when needed
- Gaining strength and understanding through adversity
- Learning from their mistakes and failures
- Forgiving themselves for their weaknesses and showing compassion toward themselves when things are difficult

Practice Emotional Resilience

You can help your child build emotional resilience by helping them grow compassionate toward themselves and gain perspective and positivity. Below are three activities to help your child build emotional resilience by focusing on the positives and practicing self-awareness.

Daily Awareness Check-Ins

A child with ADHD receives near-constant critical feedback throughout their day and lifetime. Helping your child grow aware that they aren't the only ones who have bad moments during their day can help them feel a sense of belonging and guide them into growing aware of their perspective on their day.

At dinner, go around the table and let every person share one happy part of their day and one bad part of their day. By sharing your bad and good parts, your child with ADHD grows aware of how others are impacted and will learn to accept the "bad" parts of their day because everyone else has them, too.

Using the Power of Positivity

If your child is old enough, let them write down their lists; if they are too young, have them talk to you about their list of things, and you can write them down for them. Let your child list five negative thoughts they have that are bothering them. Then, have them list five positive thoughts to replace those negative thoughts.

You can help guide your child in creating these positive thoughts by prompting them to remember where they succeeded and achieved various things. For example, if they think they aren't smart, they can replace this thought with a positive one, focusing on how they got a B on a hard test.

Building Self-Awareness

When you notice your child with ADHD negatively reacting to a situation, wait until they've settled down. When they have and if they are open to participating, let them build awareness of themselves. This exercise doesn't have to be done only after something happens. It can be practiced whenever your child feels a need to understand why something didn't go their way.

Have your child focus on the ABCs of the situation, stressor, difficulty, or obstacle. Through the ABCs, help them become aware of how they were impacted, how they reacted, and the consequences that followed. Then, help them work toward finding ways they could have reacted differently.

Let your child write down the ABCs, where A is the cause that brought about the consequence they are facing now (what happened), B is their behavior in this situation (how they reacted), and C is the consequences of their behavior. Once these have been written down, help your child recognize how their reaction (behavior) led to the consequence and brainstorm how they could have behaved differently.

This will help your child work on pre-planned reactions to situations they might regularly encounter while helping them develop problem-solving skills. For example, if your child reacted badly to a test, their behavior of not putting in the effort resulted in a bad score. Their solutions can be to put more effort into studying or asking for help when they struggle instead of skipping the work they don't fully understand. Awareness is a powerful skill that can help a child learn from their mistakes.

EMOTIONAL FORTITUDE ACTIVITY: EMOTION WHEEL

For this activity, you'll need the following items:

- Piece of paper or poster board
- Black marker
- Pencils or crayons

This activity focuses on creating an *emotion wheel* that can help your child with ADHD identify and talk about their emotions. This can help your child with ADHD improve their communication skills, social skills, and emotional fortitude.

Whenever your child feels overwhelmed and unable to describe their feelings, they can use this emotion wheel to identify what they are feeling. This, in turn, will help them talk about what they are feeling and can help you understand your child's current state of mind so you can help them through this.

Step One

Draw a large circle on the piece of paper in the black marker and divide this circle into equal parts until you have eight. In each of these sections, write the following emotions: (If your child can write, let them write down each of the emotions.)

- Happy
- Sad
- Angry
- Excited

- Scared
- Surprised
- Worried
- Proud

Step Two

Let your child decorate each of these sections the way they want to. They can color in each section according to how the emotion makes them feel, draw patterns, give colors to each emotion, or simply add drawings. Allow them the freedom and flexibility to color and decorate their emotion wheel how they want to.

Step Three

Place this wheel somewhere your child can easily find or use when needed, such as their bedroom wall or play corner. Teach your child that whenever they feel overwhelmed, they should go to this wheel and find the emotion they feel the strongest. Then, once they've identified it, they can talk to themselves about why they are feeling this emotion, or they can come to talk to you.

Impulsiveness, inattention, and hyperactivity are all factors that can impact your child's emotional fortitude and decrease their emotional awareness and resiliency. Through implementing emotional resilience activities, mindfulness practices, and stress-coping strategies, you can help your child develop the necessary skills to grow aware of and manage their emotions and emotional responses to situations and experiences. It's important that you find what works for your child to best assist and guide them. The next chapter will focus on guiding you and your child with ADHD in nurturing family bonds.

CHAPTER EIGHT

HEARTSTRINGS OF HARMONY
NURTURING FAMILY BONDS

DRESHER LARRY

The most precious gift parents can give their children is a happy marriage, especially if they have a child or more who has ADHD and has trouble making friends and keeping those friends. It also goes without saying that parenting is a big job, and when you add ADHD to the mix, it can become quite challenging. But, there is good news: helping your child with ADHD manage their symptoms lessens the stress and pressure on the others in the family. However, it is equally important for every family member to work actively toward maintaining strong bonds despite the difficulties that arise. By working together as a family unit, you strengthen the bonds that tie you and half the burdens you feel as they become shared and lighter.

This chapter will guide you in understanding how your child's ADHD can impact your marriage, sibling relationships, and extended family relationships. It will guide you in helping your children strengthen their bonds with each other, as well as strengthening your marital bonds with your spouse. Sections will be dedicated to resolving conflicts, dealing with the stress of parenting, creating family bonding time, and meditation exercises for you (the parents).

HOW ADHD AFFECTS THE FAMILY DYNAMICS

Studies have shown that ADHD impacts the satisfaction that family members experience in their daily lives. For parents, this can strain their marriage, and for siblings, it can cause a divide between siblings instead of bringing them together.

For Siblings

Siblings are impacted by their ADHD siblings. A child with ADHD puts a greater demand on parents' time and attention, which can cause siblings to be left with less time and attention. This ultimately leads to more conflict and problems within the family dynamic.

Siblings who don't understand ADHD and how it impacts their siblings can feel stressed and grow worried because they might get sick or wonder whether they are the cause of their sibling's ADHD. They might also act out in an attempt to gain the attention of their parents. They might grow angry because more is expected of them compared to their ADHD sibling, or they might even feel embarrassed to be seen with their family out in public.

Helping siblings understand ADHD and how it affects their behaviors can help them gain understanding and show compassion toward their ADHD sibling instead of growing frustrated or angry. Resentment and jealousy might even build. However, through understanding and not putting more pressure on your child than they are ready for, siblings can learn to understand and accept the family dynamics.

Parents can help balance time and attention by spending one-on-one time with each of their children—setting aside time every week for each of them to grow their relationships with each other, be able to listen to what they have to say, grow in understanding of how their ADHD sibling has been impacting them, and be able to help and guide.

Remember, teasing and fighting are normal among siblings, but pay attention to when this behavior continues and intensifies so you can act. Working on each individual relationship with your children will foster empathy, creativity, sharing, and much more between you and your children and them and their siblings.

For Parents

The demands that fall onto parents are significant. There is a constant struggle to find a balance between home and work while also managing your child's ADHD from morning to night. The demands of a child with ADHD can result in either or both parents needing to cut back on work hours—this decision can impact a family's income. The time and resources it takes leave little room for parents to have time for each other. The stress, frustration, worry, and uncertainty can lead to conflicts between parents, putting further strain on a marriage.

It's hard to keep a marriage on track when you're putting all your resources into managing your child's symptoms and helping them be able to cope with daily activities and tasks. Therefore, it's vitally important that parents learn valuable tips to help their marriage remain strong through the struggles of their child's ADHD.

- **Stop the blame game.** ADHD is neither yours nor your partner's fault. In addition, frustration caused by low patience and your child's challenging behavior shouldn't be directed at your spouse. Accept that you're both dealing with the same frustrations (even if you express these frustrations in different ways) and focus on your shared goal of creating a loving life for you and your children despite your challenges.
- **Be a united front.** ADHD shifts the entire family dynamics, impacting schedules and routines, and it's a lot to keep track of. Communicate regularly with your spouse about plans, tasks, activities, or instructions that you provided your ADHD child. For example, if you told your child to do their history homework after school, phone your spouse and let them know this is the plan so that you are both on the same page and your child won't be able to deceive either of you into wanting to do their own thing.
- **Give a little to get a little.** Placing all or the majority of the responsibilities on one parent can be too much. Instead, write down everything that needs to be done

that week and decide who will do what together. Most importantly, for each week, schedule time for you and your spouse to do something together, even if it's not something you're interested in, as long as you do it together. Then, the next week, it's the other's turn to decide what you'll be doing. This helps to strengthen your bonds and allows you to have fun together.

- **Agree with one another.** Agree on an ADHD parenting approach that you both endorse. This will ensure that each of you is on the same page regarding how you'll be praising and correcting your child's behavior. This goes hand-in-hand with communicating with your spouse regularly. This can lessen conflict and disagreements regarding how you parent your children.

IMPORTANCE OF FAMILY CONNECTION

A child who is born and grows up in a family learns the importance of values, skills, socialization, security, belonging, identity, and support. From the moment your child is born, they learn from you (their parents) through observation.

Your child (or children) looks at you to learn and understand what is right and wrong. They look to you to learn the norms and values. A child, especially one with ADHD, who will experience a lot of challenges, needs their connection to their family to help them learn the importance of controlling their impulses, doing their best to be good, and doing what's right.

Similarly, a child learns and develops motor, language, cognitive, and emotional skills from the moment they are born. Parents guide and teach a child, helping them take their first steps and speak their first words. Children learn from their siblings how to play and behave. Therefore, family plays a big role in how a child learns these skills.

Siblings and parents help a child learn to interact. Through socialization within the family, a child can observe and learn how to interact with others, make friends, seek from, and comfort others. This helps a child form meaningful relationships with those around them, giving them a sense of belonging.

A child's sense of safety and security comes primarily from their family. Since birth, a child relies on their parents to provide them with the most basic needs. As they grow and learn to express themselves emotionally, they learn to trust and find security at home, where they won't be judged for who they are but instead will find support, comfort, and unconditional love. Home (family) is where children feel safe to be themselves fully and where they can come into their identity without fear.

Raising a child with ADHD is challenging; however, family is vital in any child's development. Therefore, ensuring your child can feel safe and protected within your family will help them grow and explore, give them the courage and confidence to experience the world around them, and help them know where they can find support when needed.

STRENGTHENING SIBLING DYNAMICS

Within a home where a sibling has ADHD, conflicts can erupt because of unfairness, exclusion, competition, and avoidance. Teasing and fighting between siblings is normal. However, when a child has a sibling with ADHD, there's a bigger chance for the siblings to act out or feel like they are second to their sibling with ADHD. Therefore, as a family and parent, you need to guide your children in understanding the challenges their sibling with ADHD faces and react in a way you want your children to react.

For instance, if you and your spouse react to your child's ADHD as if it's changing your lives in a tragic way, your other children will mimic this behavior and reaction. However, if you react as if the ADHD is merely a series of challenges your child has to face and face them with grace and humor (even if it's just a drop of humor), your children will learn to react similarly. Help your children strengthen their bonds with each other by helping them understand how ADHD impacts their sibling, but also listen to how their sibling's ADHD impacts them.

To prevent your children from competing with each other or letting their feelings grow into resentment, establish an environment within your home that thrives on fairness and inclusion.

Schedule Family Activities

Fortify your children's bond and your family bonds as a whole by making time every week for you as a whole family to spend time together. If you're an active family, this might look like a hike, mini-golfing, or playing in the park, or it might look like a game night, movie night, or a cooking night. Whichever you choose, ensure that every family member gets a chance to choose what the activity will be or what movie, game, or meal will be picked for that night.

Create Inclusive Routines

Your child with ADHD will already have a routine that's fitted to them; however, keeping the whole family to a routine will ensure fairness. Set up designated roles for each child so that the playing field is leveled and each child feels like they serve a purpose within the family. For example, if your child with ADHD struggles to do the dishes, have them clean the countertops or vacuum the floor. Structure these routines and responsibilities according to each of your children's strengths so that every child feels included.

Create Outlets for Frustration

Frustration is bound to happen. Your child with ADHD struggles to control their emotions and impulses, and this can lead to negative feelings and behaviors that impact their siblings. Therefore, create a way in which your children can physically let out their frustrations instead of directing them toward their siblings—for example, a trampoline, basketball hoop, or indoor bicycle. Teach your children that whenever they feel their frustration growing, they should go let it out.

Enforce Consequences

Establish rules between your children, as you have house rules. These rules are there to ensure your children behave and act toward each other with love and care and that they are aware of the consequences of their behavior toward their siblings.

As a parent, you might unconsciously side with your child with ADHD when intervening between your children's squabbles or arguments. The best way in which you can allow your children to grow in their relationships with one another is to help them sort things out themselves. Remove the pressure on you and your spouse by setting up a consequence jar. This jar will contain chores, lost privileges, or anything else you deem appropriate as a consequence of their bad behavior toward their sibling. Whenever a child misbehaves, they need to take a paper from the jar and "serve" that consequence. This removes pressure from you and your spouse on having to intervene and allows for independence among your children.

If your son hit your daughter out of frustration, gently enforce the consequence jar and have them pick out a consequence. Then, have them serve that consequence. For example, they lose 15 minutes of TV time. Have them decide what they will do to fill the TV time they lost.

Time-Outs Are Good

Time-outs aren't just for after the incident occurred; time-outs can be used to prevent an incident from occurring between your children. Emotions can quickly snowball, and before long, someone's feelings are hurt. Separate your children for 15 to 20 minutes to allow them to settle down. Then, once they've settled down, bring them together and talk about what has them frustrated or angry at each other and how you can move forward.

And, if the situation allows, you can use their time-outs as a way for you to spend a few minutes doing what you want to do. Stealing a moment for yourself can benefit your mental and emotional wealth.

Most importantly, listen and spend quality time with your children daily and weekly. Make time for each of them—just as much as you need the support of your spouse, they also need the support you and your spouse provide them. This allows them to feel safe and secure in who they are and ensures they know they will always have a place where they belong.

STRENGTHENING PARTNERSHIP

As a parent, you have an important job; part of that job is not allowing your thundercloud to rain upon your children. In other words, do not let the frustrations, stress, and pressure you feel be felt by your children; instead, ensure that your child feels loved, cared for, heard, and safe.

Raising children is a joint adventure that requires you and your spouse to communicate, show understanding, love each other, and be willing to compromise. Raising a child with ADHD can make it even harder to find time for your marriage. It is part of strengthening your bond with your partner, but it shouldn't come at the loss of your marriage.

You and your partner need to work together to prioritize your marriage, spend time together, have fun, go on dates, and be intimate because when your marriage is strong, you both have a steady foundation on which you can parent. You both find safety and support in each other when difficult times hit. You'll support each other through the challenges, and when you lack the patience, your partner can step in. Similarly, when they lack the energy, you can step in because when you're in excess, you can help where your partner is lacking. In turn, you create a balanced system in which you both have your needs met while navigating the challenges of raising a child with ADHD.

Researchers found that parents raising an ADHD child displayed 90% more stress than parents raising a non-ADHD child (McDiarmid, 2018). This isn't surprising considering everything we've discussed up to this point on how ADHD affects the child and the family as a whole. Therefore, you and your spouse must understand that you're not alone in these struggles and that other parents of ADHD children have experienced these same struggles and strain on their marriages.

Jacqueline McDiarmid is a couple's therapist who specializes in helping parents who are raising children with ADHD work on their marriage. She noted several reasons parents find themselves seated on her couch, expressing their feelings of frustration and worry for their marriage due to the challenges they've been facing. Some of the common reasons parents found themselves seeking out help include (2018):

- Parents have been struggling for a number of years with extremely difficult behaviors and challenges before their child was diagnosed. Therefore, for a long time, they've not had the supportive resources that could have lessened their stress.
- Even the most skilled parents can find parenting their ADHD child to be extremely challenging and difficult.
- Parents feel unable to leave their house or socialize because of their child's behaviors. They are often isolating themselves.
- They receive unwanted and unsolicited advice and criticism from family, friends, and relatives on their

child's behavior and often feel like they've failed as
parents.
- Different parenting styles have been clashing, causing
  more difficulties in the marriage and in parenting
  their ADHD child.
- The ADHD diagnosis has placed unexpected financial
  pressure on them.
- They lack the space and time to work on their
  marriage because all their attention, energy, and focus
  are on their child.
- They constantly worry about their child, including
  about their child's academic performance and quality
  of life, including friendships.
- They have concerns about their other children and
  how this is affecting them as well.

It's natural to have these worries and concerns. Every parent
wants the best for their child. However, for you and your
spouse, it's just as important to work together and put in the
same amount of energy you put into your child or children in
your marriage.

Don't be afraid to reach out and receive support, whether it's
from counseling, training, or using a babysitting service so
that you and your partner can have a moment where it's just
the two of you. You and your partner need to be there to
support each other. Having time for just the two of you
doesn't make you bad parents. Instead, it shows your
dedication to each other to ensure you create a loving home
and marriage for your children.

Have regular date nights and be present during these date
nights. Let go of your worries and focus on each other. Listen—

truly listen—to what your partner has to say and share with you. Parenting is hard, so pat yourselves on the back for all you've accomplished and encourage and motivate one another to keep going. Learn to communicate and express yourself with each other, which can reduce tension, stress, and frustration and create a space in which you can be honest and open.

Learn to laugh first and grow angry second. This is fantastic advice for your marriage and your parenting. Instead of reacting out of frustration or annoyance, laugh. When your partner accidentally creates a bigger mess with the children when making breakfast, don't grow angry or frustrated because of the mess; laugh and embrace the moment. Once you've laughed, you'll realize the rest doesn't matter because love exists in these moments.

Similarly, when your child is doing something crazy, let go and laugh. Laugh with them and get inspired by your laughter to join your child on the monkey bars and experience it with them. It's easy to get caught up in life and lose sight of being in the moment with your partner and child.

Vow to date each other. The longer you're in a relationship or marriage with someone, the more everyday life seems to get in the way, or a routine is created where neither of you is really experiencing each other. Remember the first few months when you were dating and getting to know each other? Rebuild those feelings by dating each other. This means asking each other about your day, stealing a kiss, hugging, sharing a laugh, saying thank you, and doing something out of love rather than necessity. Small gestures go a long way.

CONFLICT RESOLUTION

Everything you are teaching your child, you should model. This means learning to control your impulses, behaviors, and reactions. It also means that what you teach your child about learning to soothe themselves, gaining control over their emotions, finding comfort in a schedule and routine, and all other aspects can also help you as parents manage the challenges and difficulties you are facing.

As your child needs to learn to control their impulses, breathe through them, and put their best foot forward, so do you. Learning how to resolve conflicts effectively and constructively can help your family communicate better and reduce the snowballing of conflicts in the house. It is a valuable skill that every child and adult needs to possess.

Conflict within families can arise from many things, such as a lack of communication, family duties, money, differences in values, and different goals and expectations. However, no matter what caused a particular argument, it's important to know how to prevent it from escalating and learn to minimize future conflicts.

Here are a few tips to resolve conflicts constructively and effectively.

- **Accept what you cannot control.** Learn to become comfortable knowing you cannot control other's behaviors or actions. You can only control how you react and respond. Accepting this will help you grow aware of how you respond and become aware of how you can respond better in the future.

- **Leave anger at the door.** When emotions are high, don't try to rationalize or talk through a problem, as these strong emotions will get in the way, and things will be said or done that aren't meant. Instead, set your emotions aside or wait until the anger has subsided before calmly sitting down to have a rational and constructive conversation on moving forward.

- **Be understanding of the other's perspective.** Don't only focus on how you feel but also consider how the other person feels. Also, allow them to share their perspective and actively listen to what they are saying. Understand them to gain insight into the conflict as a whole.

- **Don't assume or blame; instead, use "I" statements.** When there is a conflict, and someone tells another, "You always…" or "You never…" these statements can feel like an accusation and cause the person to shut down. However, when you speak from your perspective without blaming or accusing, it's more likely that you'll be heard. For it's better to hear "I feel hurt when you…" than "You always hurt me…"

- **Pick your fights.** Some things aren't worth the conflict they will cause. If your partner forgot to take out the bins, don't turn it into a fight. Instead, let it go. But if they do it repeatedly, bring it into a conversation and work toward a resolution. Regularly ask yourself whether it's worth the fight or whether it can simply be because it's causing no harm.

- **Always work as a team against the issue.** Don't pick a side or think it's you against the issue; it's not. Conflict is best resolved when you remind yourself that you are a team and it's you against the issue. Remembering this makes it easier to be objective and work toward a solution.

DEALING WITH PARENTAL STRESS

Parental stress is a term used to describe the stressors a parent experiences through their relationship with their child. For a parent who is raising a child with ADHD, ADHD is a great source of stress, which is why you must focus on dealing with the stress you are experiencing so that it doesn't interfere with your relationships with your children and your marriage.

Ways in which you can deal with your stress include:

- **Separate work and life as best you can.** Children are intuitive when it comes to the emotions they are feeling from their parents. Therefore, you must try to leave work stress at the door and seek out the comfort and love that you can find with your spouse and children. Don't let the stress of work spill into your home and cause disruptions.
- **Give yourself a time-out.** While your children are engrossed in their activities, take the opportunity to care for yourself by relaxing or engaging in an activity you enjoy. The clean laundry can wait another day, but your mental and emotional health is important, so take moments out of the day to spend time with yourself.
- **Connect with other parents.** The best way to feel less burdened and alone by the challenges you face as parents is to befriend other parents. This helps you

find support and understanding among others who are going through similar struggles. It also helps you to feel less alone in the struggles you are facing. Through these friendships, you can find support.

- **Be active, and remember to have fun.** Sometimes, all you need is to run the stress out while playing ball with your children or join them on the trampoline. Find physical ways to release the stress you are feeling while having fun. This helps you engage in it more often.

- **Find comfort in the things you enjoy.** Indulge in the things that make you feel happy, such as a cup of coffee or tea, a delicious brownie, or a comforting meal—maybe reading a book chapter, journaling, or painting. Perhaps you find comfort in watching a favorite film or enjoying an episode of your favorite show. You need to remember that.

- **Practice mindfulness and meditation.** You can learn other practices for mindfulness or meditation or simply adapt those that you're teaching your ADHD child to suit your situation. Practice deep breathing to soothe you when you're overwhelmed, engage in meditation, journaling, and practicing gratitude, among others. Find what works for you and do it.

FAMILY BONDING TIME

Bonding time means spending quality time with your child. Through this, you create lasting memories for your child that they will cherish. It also positively impacts their well-being and socializing as they learn honest and open communication that they can incorporate into their social interactions with classmates and peers.

Happier Children

Quality time with your children is a greater reward to them than anything you can buy that they desire. When a family comes together to spend time together, it positively impacts a child as it improves their mood, attitude, behavior, and general happiness. This can also help your child approach misunderstandings with their peers and improve their socialization skills.

Increased Self-Esteem

Children build upon their self-esteem in many ways that we don't understand. Therefore, when you spend quality time with your child, you're helping them improve and build upon their self-esteem. This increase, in turn, helps your child improve their socialization skills and interact more positively with those around them.

Decrease in Behavioral Problems

Bonding time creates a lasting bond between you and your child, which, in turn, decreases behavioral problems that may arise due to a child seeking ways to feel safe or gain their parent's attention. By bonding and connecting with your child, you create an environment where they feel safe and inspired to thrive.

Deeper Understanding

No matter how seemingly inconsequential, random, or quick the moment may be, every moment you spend with your child helps you learn more about them and grow in deeper understanding. A child also learns to adopt more favorable attitudes and attributes through these moments.

Increased Academic Performance

Your child will still experience challenges and difficulties, but the quality time you spend with them to help them learn and grow will help them feel safe. It will also bring awareness to them that no matter the possible failures and mistakes they will face, they have support and positive guidance from you. This will help your child remain motivated even though they struggle.

Family bonding has many benefits both for you and your child. So, find ways in which you can spend some quality time together. To help you, here are a few ways to increase family bonding time:

- Do chores together.
- Make dinner together.
- Create a tradition, such as movie night on Wednesdays or game night on Sundays.
- Have a lazy family day where you all relax, do something you love, and enjoy together.
- Get away for the weekend.
- Eat meals together.
- Volunteer.
- Have family meetings.

MEDITATION ACTIVITY: FOR PARENTS

Below are a few different methods in which you can practice meditation. Try each and then find the one you most enjoy and incorporate it into your daily life so that whenever you feel overwhelmed, stressed, or need a break, you can practice this quick meditation to help soothe and calm you.

Box Breathing

Find a quiet place and get comfortable. Then follow the below steps:

1. Slowly breathe in for a count of four. Let the air fill your entire chest.
2. Hold your breath for a count of four. Try to avoid inhaling or exhaling during this count of four.
3. Purse your lips and slowly exhale for a count of four.
4. Repeat steps one to three until you feel more centered and calm.

S.T.O.P.

S.T.O.P. is a powerful and basic strategy to help you grow more focused, relaxed, and emotionally centered. The acronym states the four steps that help you gain a new perspective.

- Stop what you are doing. Pause your thoughts and actions.
- Take a few deep breaths to soothe and center yourself.
- Observe the physical sensations you are feeling, the emotions you are experiencing, and the thoughts you're having. Observe them, but do not act upon them.

- **P**roceed by making a conscious and intentional choice regarding what you're thinking, feeling, and doing.

With practice, you can use this method to gain a new perspective when you're frustrated and need to readjust your tone and approach to your child.

Mantras

Mantras are short phrases, sounds, or words to help you focus, center yourself, and soothe your emotions. These can be affirmations or phrases that make you aware of your stress and frustrations and allow you to adjust your thinking or attitude toward a situation or moment. For one person, it's a simple "I am okay," but for another, it's "Not my monkey, not my circus," which helps them focus on themselves rather than trying to help everyone else with their problems, too. Perhaps you need a reminder that you're a wonderful parent and find that your son's words of "you're the greatest mom with the biggest heart" help you.

Find the phrase, word, or sound that can help calm the storm inside you and regularly remind yourself of it when you need to.

Journaling

Journaling is another great way to express your feelings, let go of stress and worries, and find perspective. Spending five to ten minutes each day writing can help you start and end the day on a positive note.

Below are a few journal prompts to help you get started. Write whatever comes to mind; don't try to overthink or scrutinize your thoughts and words. Instead, let them flow freely from you like you're shaking off the weight on your shoulders.

- What does your child do that pushes your buttons, making it hard for you to keep your cool? Do their actions or behaviors remind you of anything from your past or of yourself?
- What do you wish people just accepted about you? What do you wish people would accept about your child?
- Do I make time for myself? Do I take care of my own needs? What can I do for myself today?
- What is the hardest thing about parenting my child? How does it impact the way I feel or view other parents?
- Who can I turn to when I'm struggling and feeling overwhelmed? Who can I call when I need a supportive voice?
- My hopes and dreams for my child are…
- How do I measure the success of my children?
- What has my child taught me?
- Write a letter to yourself in which you praise yourself for your parenting and the struggles and challenges you've overcome.

Without family, we can lose our identity and place of belonging, and we feel alone and afraid. With family, we feel encouraged, supported, and empowered to take on the challenges we face, and we don't fear failing or making mistakes because we know that when we do make them, our family is behind us, cheering us on to try again.

You, your spouse, and your child need each other because each of you brings happiness, support, and safety to each other. As a parent, you feel proud when your child succeeds and praises you. Similarly, your child and spouse feel the same when being praised. Be each other's cheerleaders and support one another because that's how you get to face the challenges of parenting a child with ADHD and doing it with confidence. A confidence that grows and guides others.

Parenting a child with ADHD is a unique adventure that requires resilience and adaptability. There will be moments of uncertainty and times when you feel like you're conquering the world. Your dedication, time, and hard work will not go unnoticed. Your child will grow in their understanding of ADHD, learn how to manage it, and discover how to thrive in the world. They will transform their unique traits into powerful strengths that will pave the way for success.

We started this journey by diving into ADHD and everything it entails. This deeper understanding allows you as a parent to gain a new perspective on your child and eases some of the worries you might have been feeling. You learn that not only is it a neurodevelopmental disorder that affects their behavior, but that it's a disorder that results in deficits within their brain. You also learned to dispel those misconceptions about ADHD that might have had you feeling like a bad parent (because you're not a bad parent).

Then, this journey took you on a deep and detailed path of learning how to create an environment for your child that helps them thrive and succeed. And an environment in which they can learn and grow. Following this, you gained insights into techniques and understanding of your child's challenging behavior and the best ways to manage it. With this, you learned how to guide and help your child develop essential life skills to help them build upon their executive functioning skills. In addition, you gained insight and techniques to help your child develop their communication and social skills so they can interact with others more effectively. Lastly, you were guided on helping your child develop emotional resilience by strengthening their emotional fortitude and getting more in touch with their feelings.

The last chapter was specially crafted for you and your spouse to help strengthen your marriage in the face of these challenges and difficulties and learn to create a fair and loving home for all your children. Similarly, it focused on helping you understand the importance of spending quality time with each of your children, resolving conflicts, and learning the impact of stress on you as parents and how it can impact your children.

This guide has provided you with a lot of information, knowledge, and techniques. Now, it is up to you to take all that you've learned and put them to work. Don't wait until a "better" time because there is no better time than now.

If you're feeling overwhelmed or questioning your abilities, remember that no parent is perfect. We all make mistakes. But it's through these mistakes that we learn, grow, and better ourselves. Worrying about your child and whether you're doing everything right for them is natural. The key is to respond to these worries with love, compassion, and patience toward yourself. You're doing your best, and that's what matters most.

Never let your child's ADHD define who they are; instead, let it be part of their story and adventure. Let your child write their own adventure and path their own way toward the greatest because their challenges will inspire and motivate them to be great.

While this guide has concluded, the advice and techniques within this book will help your child reach their full potential. If this guide has helped you grow more confident in parenting your child with ADHD, help other struggling parents gain from this guide as you have by leaving a review.

REFERENCES

American Academy of Pediatrics. (2018, October 22). *Eight ADHD myths & misconceptions*. HealthyChildren.org. https://www.healthychildren.org/English/health-issues/conditions/adhd/Pages/Myths-and-Misconceptions.aspx

American Academy of Pediatrics. (2019, September 27). *Causes of ADHD: What we know today*. HealthyChildren. https://www.healthychildren.org/English/health-issues/conditions/adhd/Pages/Causes-of-ADHD.aspx

Ash. (2015, February 27). *Thirty day ADHD/autism organization plan*. Autism 360™. https://www.autism360.com/30-day-adhd-organization-plan/#DAY_26_Basics_of_Task_Management

Assistant Secretary for Public Affairs (ASPA). (2019, September 24). *Warning signs for bullying*. StopBullying.gov; StopBullying.gov. https://www.stopbullying.gov/bullying/warning-signs

Bailey, E. (2018, August 19). *Ten ways to help reduce hyperactivity in children with ADHD*. HealthCentral. https://www.healthcentral.com/article/10-ways-to-help-reduce-hyperactivity-in-children-with-adhd

Barnes, B., Whiting, G., & Amberson, S. (2012, July 19). *First, learn to listen. then, listen to learn*. ADDitude. https://www.additudemag.com/how-to-improve-listening-skills-in-children-with-adhd/

Bhandari, S. (2023, May 15). *What causes ADHD*. WebMD. https://www.webmd.com/add-adhd/adhd-causes

Bleeker, S. (2018, February 9). *Twelve powerful quotes from parents of kids with ADHD*. The Healthy. https://www.thehealthy.com/adhd/quotes-adhd-parents-kids/

Blocker, A. (2016, May 31). *The real reason why children with ADHD need structure and play*. Fuller Life Family Therapy. https://fullerlifefamilytherapy.org/4532-2/

Bonvissuto, D. (2023, March 16). *Parenting dos and don'ts: ADHD and discipline*. WebMD. https://www.webmd.com/add-adhd/childhood-adhd/ss/slideshow-adhd-parenting-discipline-tips

Brady, C. (2022, September 1). *ADHD inattention: Signs and solutions for kids*. ADDitude. https://www.additudemag.com/inattentive-adhd-in-kids/

Brown, T. E. (2014). *Smart but stuck : Emotions in teens and adults with ADHD*. Jossey-Bass.

Buzanko, C. (2022, April 4). *ADHD & stress: Three tools to use when your child is freaking out*. Koru Family Psychology. https://korupsychology.ca/adhd-stress-3-tools-to-use-when-your-child-is-freaking-out/

Buzanko, D. C. (2019, September 27). *How to manage impulsive behaviours in kids with ADHD*. Dr. Caroline Buzanko. https://drcarolinebuzanko.com/how-to-manage-impulsive-behaviours-in-kids-with-adhd/

Ceder, J. (2019). *How inconsistent parenting can cause behavior problems*. Verywell Family. https://www.verywellfamily.com/why-does-consistency-matter-in-parenting-4135227

Centers for Disease Control and Prevention. (2022, August 9). *Treatment of ADHD*. Centers for Disease Control and Prevention. https://www.cdc.gov/ncbddd/adhd/treatment.html

Centers for Disease Control and Prevention. (2023a, September 27). *Symptoms and diagnosis of ADHD*. Centers for Disease Control and Prevention. https://www.cdc.gov/ncbddd/adhd/diagnosis.html

Centers for Disease Control and Prevention. (2023b, October 16). *Data and statistics about ADHD*. Centers for Disease Control and Prevention. https://www.cdc.gov/ncbddd/adhd/data.html

CHADD. (2024). *General prevalence of ADHD*. Children and Adults with Attention-Deficit/Hyperactivity Disorder (CHADD). https://chadd.org/about-adhd/general-prevalence/

Children's Bureau. (2017, December 11). *Child abuse prevention, treatment & welfare services*. Child Abuse Prevention, Treatment & Welfare Services | Children's Bureau. https://www.all4kids.org/news/blog/the-role-of-family-in-child-development/

Chowdhury, M. R. (2019, January 22). *What is emotional resilience and how to build it? (+Training exercises)*. Positive Psychology. https://positivepsychology.com/emotional-resilience/

Clarke, J. (2022, December 3). *How is ADHD severity measured?* Verywell Mind. https://www.verywellmind.com/how-is-adhd-severity-measured-5496273

Cohen, S. S. (2023, March 10). *How to design an adhd-friendly space for kids*. Shelfology. https://shelfology.com/blog/how-to-design-an-adhdfriendly-space-for-kids/

Collins, R. (2024, March 6). *How can ADHD and ODD be managed?* Verywell Health. https://www.verywellhealth.com/tips-for-managing-adhd-and-odd-in-kids-and-adults-5207996

Cornwell, S. (2023, May 2). *Common ADHD myths*. Child Mind Institute. https://childmind.org/article/common-adhd-myths/

Cronkleton, E. (2021, August 13). *What are the differences between an ADHD brain and a neurotypical brain.* Medical News Today. https://www.medicalnewstoday.com/articles/adhd-brain-vs-normal-brain

Day, N. (2019, July 9). *Ten ways to help your child develop self-control.* Raising an Extraordinary Person. https://hes-extraordinary.com/impulse-control-adhd

Debros, K., Willard, C., & Buck, E. (2018). Easy mindfulness exercises for kids with ADHD. In *ADDitude.* https://utahparentcenter.org/wp-content/uploads/2020/04/Easy-Mindfulness-Exercises-for-Kids-with-ADHD.pdf

DeSantis, M. (n.d.). *Why kids with ADHD get bullied.* Understood. https://www.understood.org/en/articles/adhd-bullying-why-it-happens

Douglas, C. N. (1940). *Forty thousand quotations: Prose and poetical.* Halcyon House.

Edelman, G. (2022, March 7). *How to make friends: A guide for kids with ADHD (and their parents, too).* ADDitude; New Hope Media LLC. https://www.additudemag.com/how-to-make-friends-a-guide-for-kids-with-adhd/

FastBraiin. (2023). *ADHD and bullying: How to spot it and stop it in its tracks.* FastBraiin. https://www.fastbraiin.com/blogs/blog/adhd-and-bullying

Frye, D. (2021, June 24). *Messy kids room? A 30-day organization plan for children with ADHD.* ADDitude. https://www.additudemag.com/organizing-kids-rooms/

Gerten, K. (2022, October 10). *Sixteen quotes that illustrate ADHD.* Youth Dynamics | Mental Health Care for Montana Kids. https://www.youthdynamics.org/16-quotes-that-illustrate-adhd/

Hamblet, E. C. (2019, October 16). *Time management systems for teens with ADHD.* Understood. https://www.understood.org/en/articles/help-adhd-teens-create-time-management-system

How to improve listening skills in children with ADHD and autism. (2018, December 21). Special Strong. https://www.specialstrong.com/how-to-improve-listening-skills-in-children-with-adhd-and-autism/

Jacobson, R. (2020, October 22). *Why your child with ADHD has such a messy room.* Child Mind Institute. https://childmind.org/article/why-your-child-with-adhd-has-such-a-messy-room/

Jaksa, P. (n.d.). The disorganized child strategies for helping children with ADHD stay focused. In *ADHD Center.* https://addcenters.com/wp-content/uploads/2024/04/The-Disorganized-Child.pdf

Jaksa, P. (2023). *Bullying and ADHD (part one): How to help your child cope with bullying.* ADDCenters. https://addcenters.com/wp-content/uploads/2024/04/How-To-Help-Your-Child-Cope-With-Bullying.pdf

Jaksa, P. (2024, April 8). *How to improve attention span in children with ADHD.* ADDitude. https://www.additudemag.com/child-not-paying-attention-in-class-or-at-home/

Jones, H. (2024, February 9). *Do ADHD symptoms differ in boys and girls?* Verywell Health. https://www.verywellhealth.com/do-adhd-symptoms-differ-in-boys-and-girls-5207995#:~:text=Females%20-tend%20to%20show%20inattentive

Kahn, A. (2023, October 5). *Identifying your child's behavior triggers.* Understood. https://www.understood.org/en/podcasts/what-now-season-1/identify-child-behavior-triggers

Knight, B. (2023, April 12). *Housing quality may affect kids with ADHD: Study.* UNSW Sites. https://www.unsw.edu.au/newsroom/news/2023/04/housing-quality-may-affect-kids-with-adhd--study

Lebow, H. I. (2021, June 24). *How to stay productive with ADHD.* Psych Central. https://psychcentral.com/adhd/adhd-productivity-strategies-for-getting-things-done

Lesser, J. (2022, June 14). *Sibling rivalry: ADHD family dynamics, positive parenting & more.* ADDitude. https://www.additudemag.com/sibling-rivalry-adhd-positive-parenting-tips/

Li, P. (2022, October 21). *Fifty inspiring parenting quotes that get you through hard times.* Parenting for Brain. https://www.parentingforbrain.com/parenting-quotes/

Lillis, C. (2019, July 26). *ADHD triggers: What to know.* Medical News Today. https://www.medicalnewstoday.com/articles/325867#managing-triggers

Lopatin, A. (2022, April 30). *Consistent parenting in ADHD families: A 5-step plan for improving cooperation and communication.* Dr. Sharon Saline. https://drsharonsaline.com/2022/04/30/consistent-parenting-in-adhd-families-a-5-step-plan-for-improving-cooperation-and-communication/

Lorge, D. (2021). *Social skills role-playing scenarios.* The Cognitive Coach. https://www.thecognitivecoach.org/copy-of-cognitive-kids

Low, K. (2019, October 28). *Tips for helping your child with ADHD to stop, listen, and respond.* Verywell Mind. https://www.verywellmind.com/parenting-adhd-children-parenting-strategies-20543

Low, K. (2022, April 19). *Why children with ADHD need structure and routines.* Verywell Mind. https://www.verywellmind.com/why-is-structure-important-for-kids-with-adhd-20747

Maguire, C. (2022, October 28). *Build back your child's social skills in 7 steps.* ADDitude. https://www.additudemag.com/how-to-improve-social-skills-adhd-children/

McCarthy, L. F. (2022, March 30). *The weight of ADHD on your marriage.* ADDitude. https://www.additudemag.com/marriage-stress-parenting-child-adhd/

McDiarmid, J. (2018, August 20). *How AD/HD can affect your relationship*. Sydney Couple and Family. https://sydneycoupleandfamily.com/articles-by-jacqueline-mcdiarmid/help-to-manage-family-stress-when-a-child-has-ad-hd/

Morin, A. (n.d.-a). *ADHD and Social Skills*. Understood. https://www.understood.org/en/articles/5-ways-adhd-can-affect-social-skills

Morin, A. (n.d.-b). *Eight common myths about ADHD*. Understood. https://www.understood.org/en/articles/common-myths-about-adhd

Nelson, S., & ADDitude Editors. (2020, October 9). *The parents' guide to art therapy techniques & projects*. ADDitude. https://www.additudemag.com/art-therapy-projects-activities-adhd-children/

Nishanth, N. R. (2021, January 27). *Communication tips for children with ADHD*. 1SpecialPlace. https://www.1specialplace.com/2021/01/27/communication-tips-for-children-with-adhd/

Novick, I. (2021, June 10). *Parent's quick guide for disciplining kids who have ADHD*. Psych Central. https://psychcentral.com/adhd/parents-guide-for-disciplining-kids-with-adhd#adult-timeouts

Parekh, R. (2022, June). *What is ADHD?* American Psychiatric Association. https://www.psychiatry.org/patients-families/adhd/what-is-adhd

Parents guide to problem behavior. (2023, August 3). Child Mind Institute. https://childmind.org/guide/parents-guide-to-problem-behavior/

Phillips, H. (2021, October 22). *Six essential time management practices for kids & teens with ADHD*. Exceptional Mindset. https://www.exceptionalmindset.org/post/6-essential-time-management-practices-for-kids-teens-with-adhd

Ready to snap? Tips for stressed-out parents. (2021, February 10). Cleveland Clinic. https://health.clevelandclinic.org/ready-snap-tips-for-stressed-out-parents

Saline, S. (2019, September 14). *How to discipline a child with oppositional defiant disorder*. ADDitude. https://www.additudemag.com/slideshows/how-to-deal-with-a-child-with-odd-and-adhd/

Saline, S. (2021, July 7). *When ADHD drains and strains sibling relationships*. ADDitude. https://www.additudemag.com/sibling-relationships-adhd-families/

Santonastaso, O., Zaccari, V., Crescentini, C., Fabbro, F., Capurso, V., Vicari, S., & Menghini, D. (2020). Clinical application of mindfulness-oriented meditation: A preliminary study in children with ADHD. *International Journal of Environmental Research and Public Health, 17*(18), 6916. https://doi.org/10.3390/ijerph17186916

Schultz, J. (2023, October 12). *Stressors and the ADHD brain: Pandemic coping advice.* ADDitude. https://www.additudemag.com/stressors-adhd-brain/

Scott, E. (2020, April 28). *Why emotional resilience is a trait you can develop.* Verywell Mind. https://www.verywellmind.com/emotional-resilience-is-a-trait-you-can-develop-3145235

Seven reasons adequate family time is important for kids. (2019, November 19). Children Central. https://childrencentral.net/7-reasons-adequate-family-time-is-important-for-kids/

Silver, L. (2024, April 8). *The neuroscience of the ADHD brain.* ADDitude. https://www.additudemag.com/neuroscience-of-adhd-brain/

Skurat, K. (2023, March 20). *Ten ways to effectively resolve family conflicts.* Calmerry Blog. https://calmerry.com/blog/family/how-to-manage-and-resolve-family-conflicts/

Sounderic. (2023, August 2). *Understanding ADHD and communication difficulties in adults.* Sounderic. https://www.sounderic.com/post/understanding-adhd-and-communication-difficulties-in-adults

Teachers Collaborative. (2022, August 23). *Fifteen tips to help a child with ADHD develop social skills.* TeachTastic. https://www.teachtasticiep.com/post/15-tips-to-help-a-child-with-adhd-develop-social-skills#google_vignette

Vitolo, D. (2021, November 29). *Best glitter jar recipe for calmness.* Bright Little Owl. https://brightlittleowl.com/glitter-jar-recipe/

Vrouvas, M. (2023, November). *Helping your ADHD child cope with being bullied.* Study.com. https://study.com/blog/helping-your-adhd-child-cope-with-being-bullied.html

Watson, S. (2008, June 13). *Types of ADHD.* WebMD; WebMD. https://www.webmd.com/add-adhd/childhood-adhd/types-of-adhd

WebMD. (2018, July 18). *How ADHD Can Affect Your Family.* WebMD; WebMD. https://www.webmd.com/add-adhd/childhood-adhd/adhd-effects-on-family

Wexelblatt, R. (2023, October 11). *The social executive function skills that elude kids with ADHD.* ADDitude. https://www.additudemag.com/social-skills-for-kids-friendships-adhd/

Wilcox, K. (2023, October 27). *What is inattentive ADHD?* Child Mind Institute. https://childmind.org/article/what-is-inattentive-adhd/

Williams, P. (2014, July 15). *Five ways to create structure for kids with ADHD.* Parenting ADHD & Autism with Parenting Coach, Penny Williams. https://parentingadhdandautism.com/2014/07/5-tips-calm-adhd-kids-structure-kids-adhd/

Zhang, J. (2020, December 28). *Sixty-five ADHD quotes to help you understand it better.* Emoovio. https://emoovio.com/adhd-quotes/

Hallowell, E. M., & Ratey, J. J. (1994). *Driven to Distraction: Recognizing and Coping with Attention Deficit Disorder from Childhood Through Adulthood*. New York, NY: Touchstone.

McDonald, Jorie N. "40 Inspirational Quotes About Unity And Togetherness." Southern Living. Last modified April 30, 2024. https://www.southernliving.com/culture/unity-quotes.